THE JOURNEY HOME

THE JOURNEY HOME

with ELONIAS

DIANE SWAFFIELD

The Elonias Foundation

Copyright © 2023 by The Elonias Foundation

All rights reserved. No part of this book may be reproduced in any manner whatsoever without written permission except in the case of brief quotations embodied in critical articles and reviews.

First Printing, 1993. This Edition 2023.
ISBN: 978-1-7385803-5-4

Dedication

This Book is dedicated to all those people who can hear the "note" of remembering.

To all who are willing to go against the tide of opinion, against all popular belief, because they have finally woken up to that "what" they are.

Acknowledgements

This Page is dedicated to Jason and Leonie.

They have been a source of inspiration and love to me. Without their great support, I would have found my "assignment' very difficult indeed.

Whilst Elonias has been my "inspiration" to look at my life from another vantage point, JASON and LEONIE have been my strength and encouragement here upon this Earth.

To my loving husband and my dearest friend, what can I say, but "Thank You".

How little I know of my own power when I am so fearful of the attitudes of others. I care not for what others think of what I am, they will never know me.

They will only know the image of what they have created, and that is not what I am.

Therefore, I have no reaction to it because it is not a part of who I am.

That is how I need to live my life. Not through the image of others, of the image of what I believe I am, but what I am.

ELONIAS

Introduction

I realise only now that this book was planned long before I knew anything about it. The message that it carries will create confusion in many, anger in some, but a "remembering" within others. It created a "cross-road" in my life. I came to the point where everything that I believed in was challenged. The "cross-road" represented for me, the need for drastic change in my thinking and attitudes. I have to be totally honest in saying, it was not easy.

We can all look at our lives and speak about change, as if it was the easiest thing to do. However, I found it was not. I went through the most difficult and painful period of my life in letting go of so many things.

Elonias came into my life in 1986. That's my story, not his. He says that he has always been with me, but he was not able to make himself known to me until I was ready to "remember".

The journey that we have shared so far has allowed me to view my concept of life through a different vantage point. Elonias always speaks of the image that we create, that we call our real selves, which in fact, is really the illusion.

That was the difficult part. The illusion of my life. What was the purpose of it all, if my life was illusion? All that I had created, and all of the effort that I had put into my life, so that I could be a better person and help others. Was all this effort for nothing?

These were the questions that I asked as I stood at the "cross-road". Perhaps you will also ask these questions, as you open the Book and start to read what Elonias has to say.

A very vivid "out of the body" experience gave to me the courage to change. I would like to share this experience with you, so that you can perhaps understand why this Book had to be written.

This experience was in the month of November, 1991. One night, whilst sleeping, I left my body and found myself standing before three "Beings" within a very large room, They appeared within human form, and each one was dressed in a robe.

One stepped forward and gestured to the wall behind him. The wall disappeared, and the Universe came into view, and an image of the Earth presented itself. This "Being" looked at the Earth, then looked at me and said "It needs light."

I don't know what came over me, for I replied, "Surely that is your job." He looked at me and shook his head and said, "That is the trouble, you just don't believe enough. You will have to change quickly and drastically."

He continued, "Go back and tell the people upon the Earth that all has to change. Too many are caught up with self interests. That is why so many will fail."

When I awoke, it was such a powerful experience that I cried for three days. The memory of his words kept coming back to me. "That is the trouble, you just don't believe enough. You have to change quickly and drastically." I wondered what he meant.

What was it about myself that had to change "quickly and drastically". What was meant by "You just don't believe enough." I had plenty of beliefs. Which one did he mean?

I look back at that time in my life and I smile, I realise now that I was so full of beliefs that I had not left room for the belief in my own power of light. He did not mean that I, alone, could personally light up Planet Earth. He meant that we all have within us that "light" that surpasses our understanding through our conscious minds, that can create change upon this Planet.

Whilst we are looking outward to a "higher power" to solve our personal problems and the problems upon Earth, we will never be aware of the light that we have within our own Being. That experience changed the course of my life. I could never be the same again. Then Elonias came to me and said, "I cannot help you anymore with the issue of self. However, we can now begin our real work." And so it began.

Elonias has brought to me the realisation of "what" I am. I will never again be the person I was a few years ago. She has gone. And with her has also gone many friendships that could not stand the strain of the "new me". With that, I feel a sadness that I could not take these people with me. I am only left with the memories of the happy times we shared.

If this book falls into those people's hands, I wish to say "thank you". For through all of the times that we shared together, you have brought to me myself. Perhaps you are now ready to understand why I had to change, as you read what Elonias has to say. Maybe you are not.

All that which is within this Book are the words of Elonias, and not myself. At each gathering that we have had, we have taped the proceedings, and then transcribed them upon paper. This book is unedited, as he has asked.

I realise that it is not a literary masterpiece, as far as the English language is concerned, and I make no apologies for that.

All is written as it was given. There are instances where Elonias refers to "mankind" and "he", when in fact he is referring to the human population, forgive him for he is using the terms generally and does not understand the "feminism movement". If you let this oversight get in the way of the message, then you will never understand the power of "what" he represents.

You will find that sometimes Elonias is quite simple in his explanation, and sometimes he is quite complex. This is because of differing types of people that he is speaking to. For some, they need to have it simply, and for others, they require a more "in-depth" answer.

If you read this Book only through the "self", then you will never understand the value of the message. However, if you can just allow "what" you are to listen to the energy of the words then you too will awaken to the memory that you are more than you realise.

All is in reverse. Whilst the "self" controls what you should be doing in your life, then you have given over your power to the illusion of your creation. However, when you view through the "light" that you are, the reversal procedure takes place and allows you to operate through "what" you are and not "who" you are.

I would expect that this Book will challenge all of your belief patterns, as it did mine. Only when I realised that I did not belong to this Planet and to the self, that I was more than that only then did I really start to understand what Elonias was saying.

Whilst we spend all of our energy and time upon making the self comfortable and secure, we are not able to recognise the reality of "what" we are. We get caught up with the "small picture" of our stay upon the Earth, and are not able to see the "big picture" of the Universe itself and the process of evolution.

All I ask of you, as you read this Book, is to be open. If you become angry with anything that Elonias says, perhaps you need to look at why you have that reaction. If however, you have a stirring within, a "shift of awareness" and you start to recognise "what" you are, I am glad you have awakened. This Planet needs you.

Finally, I would like to thank Elonias and the Brothers of Light for trusting me with this "assignment". I hope that I have given it justice.

Diane

Foreward by Elonias

Within the pages of this Book lies a flicker of hope that the "awakening" will occur. Your Planet Earth has, for too long, been enshrouded within a blanket of fear and separation from its Creator.

Within the past lies the illusion of separation. Through your creative thought, separation occurs. Mankind creates a division through his need to have power over another through his ideas, his ideals and his need to manipulate his future, so as to ensure a better tomorrow for himself.

The tomorrow that you seek does not exist. Beyond space and time we come. We come so that you may remember "what" you are, and within the power of that "remembering" comes a renewal of light that allows all to be revealed.

Through the sanctity of life comes the analogy of the promises of a better tomorrow. However, within the moment of your "now" comes the opportunities of allowing the illusion of separation to cease.

Your Planet is divisional through a vast array of belief patterns, through social, cultural and religious representation. Whilst you do not recognise that "what" you are, you will be encased within the mire of illusion that shall take you no-where.

The scholars of life issue forth a directive that creation can be understood through scientific means. However, when one does not have all of the "pieces" that relegate creation through the knowledge factor through scientific evaluation, how can the totality of all be understood?

Your Planet operates through a reversal procedure. You view everything through the image of life and not light. You spend considerable effort in trying to regulate your life through the process of being comfortable with your worth.

You surround yourselves with the adornment of material wealth and success, within the structure of society that controls the masses through fear.

Your religions offer up nothing but useless and farcical observations of what God is. How limited that is, when viewed through your light and not your image of life.

Vast changes are now occurring within and upon your Planet Earth. Whatever you fear most will be your greatest companion and mentor.

All that you require to uphold your image of who you think you are will be taken from you, so that you can finally acknowledge that you need nothing, but that "what" you are to be revealed up unto you.

I have directed that this book be available so that all those who hear the "sound" of the light within, will awaken. Many will turn away for fear of letting go of that what they have created. And so be it.

To all who hear through my words, the power of light that they are, I say unto you, "I have returned to take you home."

Your Planet is but one step upon "The Journey Home". It is your choice whether you take the next step or not.

Contents

1	What is the Self	1
2	Relationship of Love Through Thought	6
3	Sounds of Love	8
4	What is Illusion	10
5	The Illusion of Your Reality	15
6	The Relationship of Time	20
7	Power of Thought	24
8	Memory	29
9	Wisdom	35
10	Knowledge and Knowing	37
11	Service	41
12	Healing	43
13	The Return Journey	51
14	Reincarnation	55
15	Aspects and Fragments	62
16	Duality	68
17	The Shift	74

18	Programming	78
19	The Reactor	81
20	The Regulator	83
21	Frequency Dimensional Units	85
22	Time Frames	87
23	Light Bodies	92
24	The Rotation of Compliance	94

Questions And Answers 97

25	Q&A - Love	99
26	Q&A - Pain and Suffering	102
27	Q&A - Fear of Dying	105
28	Q&A - Too Old to Change	108
29	Q&A - Mediumship	110
30	Q&A - Karma	116
31	Q&A - Responsibility	120
32	Q&A - Obstacles in Your Life	123
33	Q&A - What is Balance	127
34	Q&A - Meditation	132
35	Q&A - Symbology	139
36	Q&A - Consciousness	141
37	Q&A - Death and Consciousness	146
38	Q&A - The Past	155
39	Q&A - Ancient Civilisations	157

40	Q&A - Dimensional Energies	160
41	Q&A - Aspects & Fragments	173
42	Q&A - Fragments and Reflections	177
43	Q&A - The Note and The Soul	181
44	The Role of Elonias	186

A Dedication   191

Resources   193

Chapter 1

What is the Self

What is the self? It is a component of energy that is structured through thought and memory, operating so that it can redeem itself and remember. It is a part of the evolution that mankind exists within. All levels of life have an operating factor of programming. The self is operating right now through "who" you are, so that you can ascertain through the brain value of your conditioning.

The self is the instigator of the illusion of separation. You are more than the self. Do not re-energise the self. Do not call it the victor over circumstances, it is always the victim. It tries many ways to find the opportunity to empower itself, to feel comfortable. However, it has to become uncomfortable before it can recognise that it does not have any value here upon this Planet any longer.

When you look at self, what do you see? You see an image of what you think you are. And where did that image come from, I ask you? From the memory of your expectations that were not met through the self.

What are your expectations, I wonder? The self would not know, for it creates diversions in order to make itself comfortable.

If you look at light and you try to measure it, what do you see? I will tell you - you know it not. When you stop measuring light, then all you have left is light because the measurement is the self.

Light, let us analyse light. What is it? What colour is it? What depth is it? Where does it come from? Who knows? I do. You obviously do not because you are all using your brain to find out a measurement of the answer.

How can you say that you are unworthy, when you do not have anything to measure worthy or unworthy. It is a farcical attempt by the self to stop you knowing what you are, because you place the barrier always of your expectations of your behaviour. That is the barrier to your light. Light cannot be measured by the self. That is a fact.

It is only when you dis-engage and reach up within another expression of understanding that you acknowledge that you are light, and the illusion is the self. The self is a composite of many things which enables you to remain separate from another.

So when you speak of your unworthiness, please retract that statement, for are you not that to what I am also? It is just that you are measuring through the self, that will never know. You are here this evening wanting so desperately to remember, and you try so hard to connect. Why do you try so hard when all you have to do is just allow yourself to remember.

When you try, you have a vision of what you are expected to encounter. I speak to my Brothers of Light that you are. I connect back to the energy that you are. I do not see division here. I do not see fear here. I see the illusion that you carry with you, that it exists. It does not.

Your Earth is undergoing radical change. "About time," you say. "Let us get on with the job, as long as you do not change my life. I am willing to accept that everyone else's life will change, but do not touch my safety net of my world." Is that what you are thinking? I wonder.

Your enthusiasm staggers me. Where is your enthusiasm I wonder? Where is your enthusiasm for life? Where is the totality to remember with the essence that you are? With the empowerment of the greatness of your divinity.

Instead you seek another's advice so that you do not have to instil a forgetfulness of your responsibility. So you follow another's ideals and goals and the image of love. You become idealistic at times because you fear failure.

The Earth is upon its final cycle of its current "Program". This "Program" is the frequency of that cycle of Evolution within the time and space frame of where you are now. Therefore, many are now upon the entrance point of a new dimension of understanding that your past incarnations have not taken you beyond.

As you venture towards the entrance of a new dimension of light, you pull back because of your fear of failure. It is like someone who does not sit for an examination, in your terms, lest they do not pass it. If you do not take the examination, then you cannot fail, can you?

So some people become a little 'sick', as some people here are experiencing. Examination time is very shortly, but everyone passes if they can venture beyond the boundary of their illusion. To put it simply, within your past lifetimes, you have never gone this far before. Does that help some of you to register what you have been feeling?

The memory bank of your Being is encoded with a Program which relates to the current understanding and memory of your Planet. As your Planet starts to shift into a greater dimension of light, then you, too, will have to shift with it. It is like stepping into light before you step off this Planet, or else you will get caught up with the energy of unsureness and illusion, and I am sure you do not wish that to happen to you.

The self is reluctant to let go of that to which it has within it, or what it thinks it requires. There is an unsureness, and as each step is taken, you are measuring as to whether or not you are going to make it. As I have said before, "self" does not know how to measure because all it has within it is memory.

You ask as to how you can tell others of your understanding. To answer that, I wish to ask you again to look at the power of energy of your light and allow that to do your talking instead of your mouth. For all your mouth will do is utter farcical sentences of references to what we have spoken of, and they will look at you and scratch their heads and wonder.

I will give you an example. You will go to your friends, family, or whoever, and say "I spoke to someone from beyond this Universe," and they will look at you and say, "How strange you are, prove to me that you did." I am saying to you, "Prove that I was not here."

You cannot prove or justify anything. That is not what you are here for. You are here to re-connect to the energy of light of what you are. To by-pass the divisional frequency of illusion so that what you are is conversant through every aspect of your being. Listen to that, for it is so important.

You will never find the right words for everyone because they are full of fear. However, they cannot deny the light that you are. The light that you are is the trigger point of their remembering. Love them. Do not judge another or justify anything.

There will be many who mock you and ridicule you and you will smile and say, "But it is alright, you just do not remember." It does not matter if they remember or not. You are not here to save the Planet, you are here to reconnect to the essence of "what" you are.

Upon your world right now there is great change taking place. Within the light that you are, you will one day recognise what I am also. Those to whom are also within this room that you cannot see, they are here because of their love for you.

Do not expect great things from your Being, otherwise your Being will never understand. Allow the self to quieten down with no expectations. There is no failure. Remember that. There is either "knowing" or "not-knowing". That is all.

Chapter 2

Relationship of Love Through Thought

Let us talk about the minds of man. Let us talk about relationship. Let us remind you of what the overall effect is of a relationship.

For if you love another, you put into motion a thought of love that is met by another thought of acceptance or denial. It is love in motion to be connected through another thought of love, or love in motion to be rejected and transmuted into "no-love". Is this not the secret of relationships?

For love within thought can be divisible. It can create an expectation. It can create a transmutation, or it can create a complete denial, so when one has thought connected to love through the movement of thought, love is empty.

You have to understand thought. You try to understand love before you understand thought. If you can understand the movement of thought which contains the thought of love, the thought is not the "absolute".

It is the attachment to a person or an object or a circumstance, but it is not love. It is the movement of thought of attachment to make one feel good, and mankind bases all his relationships on this particular transference, and he calls it "love".

Whilst you are playing with the mind, you are also experiencing the game of love. When you look seriously into the mind, then you can see the implications of thought. You feel superior or you feel inferior, whatever. You need the response of another to settle the difference between superiority, which is an incompleteness of love, and insecurity, which is the reaction also of the absence of love.

It is two effects of the same. One releases the egoic aspect of the self and creates self-importance, which is relative to the release of the acknowledgement of no-love. The other is the denial of importance through insecurity, and one is also having the same movement of thought.

If you love me through your thought and I do not respond appropriately to equal what your expectations are, do you remove your love? Do you remove your thought and replace it with another thought of the incompleteness of love until I react wholeheartedly with my approval of your love to the dimension of thought of expectation that you carry towards me.

Therefore, together, we shall exchange thoughts of love as long as the self is able to respond to the expectation. Is that not what you call the relationship of love? However, if you look at love in totality, it has no movement of thought at all. It is all encompassing love. It allows and transforms all that it comes in contact with.

Chapter 3

Sounds of Love

Have you ever listened to the sound of Love? Have you ever waited to hear the sound of Love? Have you ever needed to register an experience of savouring each moment with the sound of Love? For the folly of mankind rests upon this interpretation of the sound of Love.

Is it within the laughter of the children? Is it within the newborn baby's cry? Is it within the greeting from one to another? Is it in the sunrise or sunset that is watched upon a mountain? Is it the sound of raindrops that fall against the window pane? Where do you hear your love? Where do you hear the sounds? From whence do they come?

When love is registered through the outward sounds, it is only a reflection of what mankind interprets through his response of love. For love has no form. How can a blind man feel love from the sunrise and sunset? How can a woman who cannot bear a child find love from the new born babe?

How can the man within the desert listen to the raindrops upon the windowpane? How can one who does not have another to greet them, where is love for them?

For surely love is sounded through the greater recognition of the knowing all is one, complete, and that there is no darkness within the light. There is no sorrow and no pain. There is no joy, there is no laughter, but there is more, and that is in the acknowledging with the innermost part of your Being the sounds of silence that have no form and no outward sound of thought. It is a totality of knowing that all is together, all is one and all is love.

To remember is not to know, it is to recall, and that is memory. To release the memory of love is to acknowledge a partial remembrance and acknowledgement according to the current inference of what you are registering, and comparison is always given from the past to the now.

As you silently project it into the future, you call it expectation of love. It does not have a sound that is registered with the Inner Being, but instead has a sound that is acknowledged by the outer, which is the self.

So when you look at the totality of love through the note, through the sound, through the vision, through the response, you are only the unlimited-ness of love, No form, no thought, no memory, just love.

The sound of love is in the complexity of the simplicity of all - and that "IS".

Chapter 4

What is Illusion

Windows of the mind. Windows of the mind is where you are within your estimation of life. Your vocabulary has been enhanced with executing new ways of understanding.

Can fact be operational within illusion? Or does illusion create a fact?

What is understanding when one is looking through the window of one's mind? A joyous encounter with illusion. A re-created connection to illusion through great verbal satire equals illusionary fact.

Let us look firstly at illusionary fact. What is fact when viewed through the consciousness of illusion? You are searching through that to which has been given to you and verbalising it through illusion, which is your mind. You either know it or you do not. You either register an awareness of its delivery or you do not. There is no fine line that can be encountered.

When one looks at understanding, it is an illusionary definition at that point of consciousness. You are well rehearsed with consciousness. Does consciousness create a fact or does a fact create consciousness? An interesting observation of illusion.

You might ask, "But how can knowing be recognised without first going through the transmutation of illusion?" It cannot, for through the illusionary concept of time, you are endeavouring to recognise the reality. By-passing the Program that you inherited when first you took on form.

You have encountered a directive input of relativity through recognising that to which was not real. The illusionary conquest of fact has brought you to this moment of investigation. There is a restlessness when one endeavours to remember through visual perspective through doubt and fear.

You wrestle with your imagery of your life and attempt to ascertain what is reality through the brain space of your consciousness.

You expect to find all that which you need to uncover. Who said that you need to uncover anything within the imagery of your expectation? Who said the light had been turned off? Do not think. Follow what I am saying with the energy of knowing. You have not missed anything, for there is nothing to miss.

Whilst you are looking for something to uncover, you create an image of expectation of what it possibly could be. So you create an imagery of "no-love", so that you can fit it into your life, and you call it "completion and love."

You are going the opposite way by expecting that you are "no-love" creating an opportunity to place love where love is not. However, that is the illusion. "No-love" does not exist within the imagery of what you think you are not. You think you are not love so no-love is created so that love can be placed within it.

You have woven the imagery of this journey through matter, expecting to uncover no-love. Replacing that to which you have created, which is the emptiness, to replace the image of love. Whatever you are looking for you will find. When you do not look for anything, it finds you.

Let us look at "awareness" what does that mean? What is the requirement to equal awareness? When one "Is", it does not need awareness because is a measurement of what is not the "Is".

You go around in circles, expecting with your illusionary movement of recognition of illusion to locate "non-illusion". You are looking for facts through your appraisal of your recognition of "no- light".

Your analysis is quite brilliant, as analysis goes, which is nowhere. Analysis is the measurement of the requirement of awareness, remember that. When there is no need to be aware because one knows, there is no separation value through illusion.

When you enquire through acknowledgement, it is a measurement, is it not? Acknowledgement is the measurement of what one requires to be aware of. When you do not acknowledge, but you know, there is no response.

It is just an absolute connection to the frequency that is available. Remember that. You are within an illusionary frame of reference which is a physical manifestation of reference, but you are not really occupying that space and time at all.

You are within an illusionary journey. The brain cannot cope with that. It will say it does not compute. Therefore, I do not speak to the brain. So you will shut down your brain and you will now switch into the higher frequency that you have available, but you had forgotten.

As you switch into the note that you really are, we will communicate. Still working through the brain, but by-passing its evaluation. You will question through your brain, but re-connect to the energy that you are, so that it can re-connect to what I am and allow the brain then to be stimulated with the greater acceptance of what you are.

While you enquire of illusion, all you will find is all you expect to find. When you enquire with your knowing, you therefore have to bring about a recognition of that knowing within a verbal sense of the brain.

Instead of the brain accepting it and analysing it through past memory, it will then by-pass through the brain into the higher order that you are, transferring what is already within it back into the brain without any analysis.

Releasing the imprint of knowing within the memory of not-knowing. To put it simply, to allow the remembering to be acknowledged by the brain but not allowing the brain to do the remembering.

When you register the frequency of life, you have two options. You can continue to operate upon the energy of illusion, which creates conflict, and become caught up with trying to find the correct method to equal what you expect of yourself, in your analysis and how to implement that. Or, you can connect to what you really are and allow that to be the instigator of all your enquiry through illusion.

So there are two operating factors that are available, but you are only aware of one option and that is trying to uncover through illusion that to which has never been lost anyway, because all it does is create more illusion of what you think you don't have.

Chapter 5

The Illusion of Your Reality

Let us discuss the Foundation Stone of Light. Let us look at the value of the Foundation Stone that you are.

To use the term of reference, Foundation Stone is a base upon which to place all other examples that you have of what light could be.

The base itself is the frequency that you are, and upon that base is created a fabrication of what light could and should be. Within the destiny that you are, lies a multitude of examples of relating to what you are creating upon your Foundation Stone that is your reality.

You are wondering, are you not, as to why you cannot fully connect to the frequency of light. That is because you are only relating to what you have created, which is the fabrication that you have woven to what light could and should be, instead of reaching into the Foundation Stone itself, which is the base to which you draw your knowing from.

Let us look at it as a "core value system". From the core it reaches out into the connection of your lifestyle upon this Planet. "What is light?" you say. "What meaning has it for me?" To the "me", it means nothing, it is just another barrier of self expression that one cannot relate to whilst within the self.

It is the frequency that is very apparent which is the Foundation Stone of Light itself. It has had the movement through many Time Frames, in order that each Time Frame can connect to the new fabrication that has been built around it in the resultant image of that frequency.

Through varying Time Frames, one starts to really understand that the illusionary movement relegates to itself an unpredictable connection to its creative magnetic field. The base that you are is the connection to the reality that you are, which is the highest, I repeat highest in your terminology of frequency of light. All else is a reflection.

You have created upon your base through the self images that you have, an interwoven fabrication of idealism regarding what you regard as your fortitude of light. Whilst you reach within the fabrication. you are only reaching within the reflection, instead of the absolute frequency that can be drawn upon. Thus creating more illusion and more fabrication of what you consider is the reality of all.

From where do you draw your light? Where does your light reside? I will tell you this - it does not reside within any Time Frame. They are only the reflection of the reality. Each reflection being responsible for creating and connecting back to that which it relates to within that frequency, in that moment of inference of its relativity, not as its inner, I repeat inner frequency of reliability.

How can you question light? You can question what you have created, and then you will create more for your brain to question. You are in-sensitive to the light that you are to the reactionary stream of your reference of what your expectation is of your behaviour.

You say that you are working with energies but I do not think that you are. You are looking at energies and trying to see energy through the brain and then remembering it is not the brain that you should be looking through, It is the Inner Being that should regulate the requirement of acknowledgement.

You query through the movement of elimination, so that you can come up with something that is close but not necessarily right. If you use the movement of elimination, then you only have a few movements, and that is within the boundary of that scale.

If I use the example of bringing unto you one that you had never connected to, how would you understand the connection of that light to yours? You would have no reference point through the consciousness, because all of your references are in accordance to the frequency that you believe you are.

Beyond the Time Frames of your observation, is the reality. You use your connection through memory and the elimination process to establish a connection to light. Then you can give it a name and feel clever or not too clever, according to your interpretation of your "hit or miss" situation.

What if you removed form altogether? You are aware of the mission of light that has no mission at all. It is the uncovering, is it not? The mission is only within this Time Frame, but not within the reality of all.

So you are relating within a Time Frame for your references, and so illusion is within your Being for the recognition to take place of illusion or non-illusion, according to the foundation that you have connected to which is not the base, but the fabrication that you call the Foundation Stone.

The reality of the Foundation Stone does not need to be built upon, for it is the fullness of the all. There is no measurement of time or space. There is only the ultimate connection of your knowing, So if you wish to work with energy, then you work with the uncovering of illusion, going beyond the frequency that you are.

I will tell you something .. "The imagery of Light is the illusion of knowing." The imagery of light is the illusion of knowing because light has no image, Knowledge is the indicator that you know nothing.

With one sentence of knowledge comes a thousand memories, all illusionary of course. When you discover they are illusionary, then you fragment them again into reality, which is another aspect of illusion. If you do not get it right the first time, then you wish to change it until you do get it right. One sentence can manifest millions of memory cells within the brain, all competing against each other. Depending upon which day one draws from is the imagery of that particular sentence. Then looking at it upon a different day, and have a different concept altogether in accordance to what one is relating to.

There are progressive laws of light, and you may query as to why light has laws. It is the step ladder to become aware of the renewal of faith that allows one to fully immerse oneself into the fullness of reality and not through the fabrication of what light is.

So one has to go through varying transition stages, and cannot pass that point unless the law is fully appreciated and accepted. When you can draw from the waters of Remembrance, that is when the inner realisation of totality of light, and not fabrication of illusion of light can take place.

Have a look at yourselves. Are you not aware of the aloneness before the reality can be fully recognised, else you will continue to draw from the restructured aspect of your awakening and that is your illusion of what light is.

You will hide behind the creative truth of what your visualisation of light is. Light is only apparent when there is nothing else left. Nowhere to hide. No attachment, just a total release, then the laws of light will show you the way through the total illusion of creation by bringing about each law, which is a symbolic reference of a disconnection of one frequency into another.

The laws that have been given are really barriers to enable one frequency to exercise complete denial of its need to be fulfilled. That is an interesting statement, is it not? Light does not need to be fulfilled, so we are looking at evolution through many varying forms of commitment of recognition. When you can be delivered from this Planet, and recognise the "Absolute" that you are, do you think that is your totalness of what you are?

It is not. It is only an image. When you do not require to hold onto your image of your "Absolute", the natural laws take place, and therefore you release yourself from the fabrication of light into the next fabrication of light, which is a greater awareness of reality. However, still not the "Absolute" of the "Absolute".

Chapter 6

The Relationship of Time

Let us talk about the future. Let us not talk about the past, and as you register, "What is the future, what does it mean?" Let us look at that, and let us enquire together about the energy that is not as yet accessible to the consciousness.

When you look at time, you look at the reference of what your vision, your hearing and all of your senses have ascertained as to being Reality, and that is the measurement of time. So when one speaks of the future, there is a measurement of time to the day that has not as yet arrived, whether it be on the morrow, or one week, one month, one year or one decade.

Still a measurement of time, and when one has a measurement of time, they have a measurement of expectation. How can one understand the future when they are measuring it by the past? So therefore, if you measure through the past, which is thought and memory, you will never go into the future. The future never exists, because it is always the past.

The energy of the future is already present. I am sure you understand that, because that is the energy of what I am. If I can exist, and you are relating to that existence, what allows the past and the future to be possible, to be related to?

Are you in fact measuring the energy of what I am into the past of what you are? Or are you, in fact, listen to this very carefully, not within the past at all, but in fact within the energy of the future, looking back to the past of the way it was. Therefore, placing a thought within the past to allow the past to be experienced as if it was the future. Listen to what I am saying.

How many people consider their life within futuristic analogies and possibilities? Or do they in fact live within the past past. Strange words, but very viable.

So we have the people upon your Planet trying to be responsible, inventing things that take them into the future. However, all they are doing is using the energy of the past to implement a possibility of what the future could hold.

They are, in fact, using form to implement the future rather than using frequency. When you look within form and regulate form to take a new image, that is not the future. That is another image of form.

When one speaks of the future in grandiose terms, and speaks of the future as being of love and peace and harmony, it is not possible when one takes the energy of that moment, of that evaluation of the future, into the future itself.

That is the bridge from one moment to another, that allows no change, no frequency of evaluation of light and love, so why should the future contain light and love when it is evaluated from the past. They have taken an image of what they think it will be into the future, so there is no change, they just live within that same image, but the future does not exist. It is still the past, because the energy is still the same.

You can change your calendars and call it the future, but it is not the future, it is another era, another month, or whatever, but it is still not the future in the sense of the word.

The future is only a word that is used to measure one movement into another, but it is still contained within the same energy of time, and from where I am looking from, it is still the past. I hope you are following me.

Only when the energy connects to that what I represent and where I am, would it be within the future, because it resonates to the note which is different to that which it has already been. Or else the same notes are being played, a different day, a different year, same notes, same measurement of time through memory and thought of the past.

So when we look at the future, we look at an "energy renewal faction", and not of another day or another year or a decade even, because that future does not exist because it gets caught up again with the past. The past has joined up with another day, but the same frequency is being emitted.

Therefore, when one looks at the analogy of the future, they need to recognise a different reaction to what the future represents.

Many ask, "When is the light going to come? I am waiting. I have time, I can wait a little longer. If you say it is coming, I shall sit here and wait for it." There are so many who are "waiting", but they are waiting in the past for the past to catch up. Surely you can see that.

To all who are waiting for the light to come, I ask you, "Are you still waiting for the past to catch up, or are you waiting for the future?" Where are you my friend? The future you will never see because the future cannot come to you, you have to go to the future.

Chapter 7

Power of Thought

Whilst recognising that "original thought" is, in fact, creation, have you really investigated the power of thought through your interpretation of what thought is?

When you look at the Earth, you see the result of thought. How can you completely recognise what the Earth totally is unless you can register the value of thought. Has thought value, or does thought have no-value? If you look at it as value, then the inference is that one becomes aware that thought allows the recognition of the original thought.

If you looked at the no-value of thought, then you transgress and transmute all thought into the parity and collectiveness of what you respond to as original and total thought. Does thought therefore have a value in fragmentation, or should all thought be followed through so that the original thought is totally revealed without any further thought being attached to it.

Form upon the Earth is a part of a mechanism of thought creation, and all thought relates to thought. Can thought relate to no-thought? When there is a space where thought is not, what will thought do? Does thought have to respond to another thought? If you removed all thought from the original thought, there is nothing to connect it to, therefore, it doesn't evaluate itself because there is no other thought than the original one.

Are you, each one, the original thought, or are you the result of thought? Think about that one. If you are the original thought, why then are you a transmutation of thought, which is a fragmentation of a no-thought.

Within your remembering of the value of no thought, can this be possible, for thought to fragment itself so that it can know?

I will give you an example of what I mean. When you respond to the fragmentation of another's thought, and you meet it with another thought of your creation, thought meets thought. What is created? More thought. Is one thought able to completely annihilate another thought without a further thought being issued?

You speak of the world of thought, and yet you need to understand what is thought. Where does thought come from? Not the original thought, which is creation, but the memory of thought, which is the fragmentation and transmutation of thought through the lesser vehicle of expression through mankind's interpretation of knowing.

The original thought is that which has never been looked for. One also is aware that one issues an ultimatum that the self has to resolve the knowing, whilst the physical body, which is the result of the fragmentation of thought, is allowed to have the power. Then all thought is a fragmentation of the original thought.

My question to you is - Can you go beyond the physical thought so that the original thought can be acknowledged while still within a physical vehicle?

Whilst you are upon the Earth, with the expectation of being within matter and acknowledging that matter is solid, whilst this is operable through the brain, then one is not able to see that within oneself are dimensional frequency units that vibrate to other levels and Programs at all times.

The physical body is a manifestation of fragmented thoughts, which is nothing to do with the original thought. Is is the duplicate of fragmented thoughts, but is not the original fragmented thought. That will make you have another thought. Further your investigation without allowing the fragmentation to be uncovered through the enquiry of the original thought, which is already within life.

It is counter-productive to create an illusion of original thought without first, listen to this, transmuting all thought which has fragmented, of which you are a duplicate of. The journey to which you are on, if you wish to understand your past experiences, throws forward in your time, a reflection. You are now a reflection of the past. You are therefore not the fragmented thought of creation, but a duplicate - a reflection of that fragmentation through what you call "time".

Whatever the yesterdays have produced, throws the image into the tomorrows. You are the result of yesterdays. This is a reflection of your fragmentation.

You ask how do you stop the fragmentation, and my answer is, by not looking for the original thought. If you look for the original thought, how can you see it through the shadow of the reflection of the fragmentation of thought?

How does a blind man see the sunshine until first the eyes are able to reflect the light. Through the barrier that is created, one cannot see the light. How can truth be revealed through a fragmentation of awareness? One has to transmute the fragmentation before you can totally be aware.

Whilst you call the fragmentation the truth, you incorporate a greater dimension of fragmentation to the thought value of truth, which is not the reality, but is instead the superficial reaction of the reflection, which is the duplicate, and one calls that truth.

How can you see the total knowing of, for want of a better word, the "IS", if you are still encased with fragmentation and the duplicate of fragmentation that you are now. The original fragmentation is what you would term the "knowing" within the dimensional value of your created Universe.

Knowing is a fragmentation of what you call the "IS", and whilst you are looking for the original thought, you are not able to transmute the fragmentation because you are adding more fragmentation of thought.

You need to become aware of what fragmentation is, and by acknowledging that, one transmutes the fragmentation, not to find the original thought, but to be aware totally that the fragmentation is able to be transmuted through the aspect of the knowing.

Upon the dimension that your brain resides, you are not able to comprehend what is a fragmentation of original thought. It is not possible, You are programmed to transmute only. You are not programmed upon this Planet to locate the original thought.

Chapter 8

Memory

When you speak of personal issues, you speak of the separateness of collectiveness, and when you speak of the separateness of collectiveness, then you are not speaking about memory at all. Instead you are speaking about fragmentation. The responsibility of memory goes further than you realise, and whilst each one has their own memory, then you get a fragmented response.

When you sit within a room discussing memory, each one is responsible for their fragmented response to their particular memory. However, if you look at memory - the whole memory, a particular event, then all may relate to the fragmented response through different and individual characteristics of memory through past action.

What is memory? Is it an aspect of the collectiveness memory that all can reach within for their own personal recollection of memory? Then surely this is a fragmentation of memory in accordance to a personal account of memory.

So memory, which is a form of reference, is drawn upon by memory in different ways. Is this memory a singular memory, or is it a collective one? If you ask the person that is reviewing the memory, they will call it the whole memory, for they do not relate to another who also has memory, which brings it into a singular thought through their own personal account.

Where is reference to memory? You speak of the collectiveness of memory, and yet you speak of it as individual memories within a memory, You see the Earth with memory in and around it, and you call it the "collective consciousness" through thought that has created memory. When you draw upon memory, you refer to it as a singular one and you give it form to make it your own memory.

If you have memory of fear, then fear takes upon itself many forms, but it is still memory of fear. So you wish to transmute memory, or do you wish to transmute fear, within singular that is your fear or fear within the whole of memory? You review memory still as separateness of your own personal memory, and yet you speak of memory of the collectiveness and you do not understand. So each one seeks to transmute personal memory and not memory of the collectiveness.

Let us look at fear. Let us look at the wholeness of fear. Fear is within memory. We are speaking of the collectiveness of memory, which is fear. The form that is taken from individual responses to memory of fear is separate, but the memory of fear is the collectiveness that is generated by separateness of thought. Reverse it. You look at fear and you look at the individual response of memory of fear. Fear is fear. Whether it be your fear or another's. There is no separateness of fear, except within the individual response and form that is given to fear.

I wish to speak of the collectiveness of memory, and to look at your personal account of memory, which is the same, and yet when separateness enters to give it form, then it is drawing upon the collectiveness of memory, creating separateness. Through your life you speak of memory as if you own it, but you cannot own memory because you have drawn a portion of what it represents into a circumstance, then you call it memory.

If you look at the collectiveness of memory, there is no separateness. Collectiveness is the whole, it is not singular and it cannot be owned. Personal memory is really an aspect of memory, which is fear, which is joy, which is hunger, which is doubt, and so on. You are still within memory. You are conditioned to speak of memory within a singular form and you give to it reference through circumstances.

Fear is the collective memory, and to draw upon the collective memory is to give a singular example through your reaction and experience, and you call it memory.

Let us use your experiences of memory. You come together and you discuss your reaction to memory, and you call it memory. It is not memory, but a fragmentation that you have allowed form, but it is not memory. Fear, joy, doubt, whatever memory you have is one memory. When you feel fear, that is fear, and all living things acknowledge the memory of fear.

However, if you look at it as the fullness of memory, then you do not allow another to understand what your memory of fear is.

So you guard your memory and respond to it through self-pity, through anxiety, through illness, or whatever, and you look at each other and you say, "But you do not understand what fear really is! You have made it a personal memory and you have coloured it to allow yourself to hide from reality.

You may ask, "Where does fear originate from?" My answer is, it originates from thought. The thought is fear, but the reaction of fear is fear. When fear which is with the soul memory of living things, which is created by thought, manifests itself in singular form, it fragments and is then duplicated by a reaction. Hence the collectiveness of fear is expanded.

Whilst you speak of fear as a privately owned experience that no other could understand, you put it with other effects to create an illusionary effect of what fear is, and some call it "love". Take away the illusion, and you are back to the memory of the collectiveness, which is fear.

For example, I love you. I do not wish you to converse or be with anyone else. Stay by my side, because I love you and I wish to protect you.

However, that is not love. It is fear of rejection, and one colours the memory with illusion and calls it something else. They then give it the name of love. So when someone leaves the side of another, they can become vindictive because they feel rejected. Some time passes, and they then meet another, but they have memory of fear, and so increase what they call love in the protectiveness.

This also means children. I love you my child as long as you meet my needs. As long as you do things that society expects, and it is because I love you that I do not let you do other things. I remember the past rejection, so I instil greater love so that I am not rejected. Is that love or is that fear?

So the collectiveness of fear is the underlying display and cause of memory. When you really look at it, there is not too much within memory. There are only a few things within the collectiveness of memory, but are given other names.

What if I told you there was only one thing within the memory of collectiveness, and that is LOVE, and the fragmentation of love is given the illusion, and that is "fear", which is a major component of another fragmentation which is sorrow, doubt, greed, and so on.

If you look at love as the main component of memory, and the breakaway of the lack of, is fear, then break fear down into other aspects that are too many to count. Yet you look at memory as being so complicated, but it is only because form is given to it through illusion of thought.

Thought itself is illusionary in accordance to what is called fear. Simple, is it not? Is this not the collective consciousness that all write reams and reams of paper about to make it complicated for scholars of life. It is so easy.

Remember that fear is born through love, You have love and you do not have love. So you have what you call the positive and the negative. If you wish to call love the positive and no-love the negative, you can. From the negative comes fear, and illusion is created, and it is called love, but it is not love. It is fear.

You question if you can transmute fear by recognising that it is really love. Fear is the negative aspect. It is the no-love of love, but it is still love. The illusion is that there are absolutely "billions" of memories to be transmuted. The only memory is love and no-love. You have in fact by-passed, in your terms, billions of memories, so you can get to the reality of the collectiveness memory, which is simply "love".

What if I told you that the collectiveness of memory, which is the singular form that mankind gives it, is the creator of form of the Earth. You call it "God", and yet is it not the creative thought of illusion, and that is fear. You manifest the illusion that you have created. That will make you think.

The creative illusionary power, which is the power that you give the creative mind, gives to you form upon the Earth. Is this not different than you would have thought? Does it not give you back control of life? Are you not what one calls "God?" God is the creator, and this is what you are.

However, when one sees God as not of the creative mind, but of the "Absolute", then one reduces the power of the creative mind into the Absolute, which is life. Hence the power of the creative mind is lesser and the wheel of life is extinguished.

Chapter 9

Wisdom

The Wisdom that you seek has no beginning and no end, and as you struggle upon the by-ways of life, you wonder what does it all mean?

The circumference of the Earth has relegated to you, each one, a place upon the molten ball that is spinning through the eternal sky, and you call this place "home".

You call this place "Earth" that is real, and that has upon its surface the direction to Wisdom.

All that you relate to is seemingly endless in regards to your perspective of your illusionary Wisdom. You wonder, as you venture along the pathway of your creation, where do you expect to 'be going? Where does it lead you?

If you look at the symbolic aspect of it, you will see that all pathways are intertwined, criss-crossing at various places in order that you find companionship with another, who is seemingly oblivious to what life totally holds for you.

For each is upon their investigation, through the self-image they have created, and each looks for Wisdom within the words of another. Within the actions of another, and within the Sky that holds the mystery of things so endless.

Some dig soil for artefacts of past civilisations to give to them the clue of life, What is so mysterious about life? What is one searching for?

Somehow it always seems to be out of reach, for when one thinks that they have found it, it changes its form and becomes not what one would envisage to be the result of Wisdom.

You live upon a ball of rock that is spinning through the eternal sky. How can Wisdom be upon it, when all that stand for Wisdom are not upon it.

It is only knowledge that you will find through another's interpretation of Wisdom.

So be it.

Chapter 10

Knowledge and Knowing

When one wants to know, one does. There is no question involved. It is the releasing of knowing into the fabric of thought.

When you enquire with thought, you are enquiring into the imagery of what one is enquiring into.

You wish to investigate fully the reason for all. You are not able to touch the knowing through your investigation, and so you clarify through your thought and use discussion, which is only to clarify each other's thought in the appraisal of the subject at hand.

You will be wondering about the "knowing" and if one's knowing is the same as another's. What is true knowing you may ask. How can one differentiate between knowing and knowledge, which is the result of creative thought.

When one flows into the stream of knowing, there is no shift from the inner realisation of truth to the oneness of knowing. The brain, which registers the memory through thought, is instrumental to one's diverse thought stream of renewal of another's ideas through their own interpretation, and through their own point of interest.

However, the knowing has no shift of point of reference as knowledge does. It cannot be described by mere human words or descriptive platitudes so as to increase one's excitement of appearing to know. There is no thought registered, so there can be no description of it.

When one is aware of knowing, one ceases to acknowledge the outward influence of life, and does not flow with the current misconception of imagery. For knowing does not have any connection to the imagery story that so many are so good at.

I will give to you an example. You are currently enquiring into "What is the soul?" When I ask you why do you need to know, your answer is that you are trying to understand evolution. However, you are trying to be intellectual with your knowing.

Are you aware of the sound of the soul? Are you aware of the energy of the soul, totally and utterly aware? If you are, then you do not ask, but you know. You know that the soul is the one soul. It is no different from one to the other here within this room. It is the one sound coming from the Absolute Light of the thought of creation. The one soul is then fragmented through the instigation of more thought, from the Planet that comes through the Program that is sent by the Higher Mind, How can you understand that,when you do not know it?

You will then ask me scores of questions so that your intellect can gain more knowledge, but it is not the knowing. It is the knowledge that is intellectual to make your case in your appraisal, so that you share it with others, who will fragment it through their evolutionary mind and find a home for it through their interpretation.

The knowing is lost, it is a furthering of knowledge. Do you see what I mean? If you do not, then I say unto you to instigate a complete knowing, then you have no further questions, for it reveals itself totally. It is the asking of the question that fragments the knowing.

So, when you look at what you call "investigation", it is an openness of awareness. It may or may not have a form. It may be a generalisation of thought image that each one has, and that is called investigation on an outward movement through the verbal sense. However, true investigation has no words. It is a revealing moment of knowing.

When the brain is stilled, all can be aware that the knowing is in the revelation of the all encompassing Mind, which has created this Planet of thought.

Many fall into the trap of allowing the brain to do the knowing when the brain is only the centre of evaluation. So when discussion is present, nothing is understood unless the revelation of knowing allows itself to be recognised, otherwise all you are doing is using your intellectual capacity to analyse and re-create through imagery of what you believe it to be. There is no truth in that.

So verbal discussion has to be kept to a minimum to allow the space of the "inner" to function, and allow the knowing to manifest itself, through the mind into the consciousness, without re-creating it and changing it through discussion. So discussion should be done gently and slowly and carefully, without any definition or imagery of truth.

Allow it to instigate the awareness of the knowing to reveal itself into the consciousness, instead of the intensity of discussion to find a reason for intellect to manufacture a reality. That is what happens too often.

When one tries to manufacture the state of awareness, one receives a manufactured awareness, which is thought induced, and has no credibility beyond the credibility of the original thought, The "Program" of the mind is a state of being that can be tapped into at any time, but cannot be tapped into by a manufactured state of awareness.

Through the clarity and stillness of absolute thought, one becomes the clear channel, so that, through the mind of the creation that this Planet is responding to, the Program can be revealed. The same program, because there is only one soul.

All can tap into that when they are receptive, not to their creative thought forms, but are truly awakened to the knowing that the transition of frequency of knowing is available, without any effort being made.

Chapter 11

Service

Service, what does it represent for mankind? It is an age-old question that religions and doctrines have added and subtracted to and from. What is Service, and why does one need to have it?

Let us look at Service, or could one say "self- service". The desire to serve, is that not what we are looking at? Then ask why you have a desire to serve. Perhaps you would say that it is because it is expected that you duly give action to your desire, so that mankind may be raised from the mire of misunderstanding.

What if, through Service, one has misunderstanding? Does that implicate more misunderstanding? In seeking the desire for Service, one then compounds ones ideas with ones intent to give that to which one believes in, However, if you do not have an environment that equals the desire and intent, then one has restrictions upon oneself, Within your environment of Service, "self-service" that you call "God service", you are ready to stand firm for "self-service".

However, Service in its truer sense needs no desire. It allows itself to reveal itself in an output of love, seeking no commitment, no dutiful expression, it seeks to reveal itself through love. You are desiring to be of Service through love, but it is not possible. That is where mankind makes his greatest mistake.

For the desire for Service has nothing to do with love. When you desire to serve, you are measuring against another. Trying to equal an opportunity, so that others may feel satisfied with what you have to give. Equalling your self satisfaction, so that you, in turn, can go forward and know that you have been of assistance.

Service becomes fragmented through your desire to operate through the need to serve. Service is operable at all times through no desire and no need to inflict upon another their need for your Service.

For Service is automatic when you do not have a need or desire to have it, because that is a self induced action. It automatically operates on "Natural Law" basis by the frequency that you are, that reflects in the action that you have. Do not create an action. An action is automatic, A response to natural Service.

Chapter 12

Healing

When you speak of healing someone, I wonder if you have really fully understood what healing means. Many people are drawn to exercise "healing" upon another, but I wish to ask you a question. "What do you wish to heal? Is it the body? Is it the mind? Is it the emotions?" Or perhaps you could lump it into one fragmented response of the Soul.

Let us look firstly at disease. You may ask if disease is pre-determined for the individual before they came upon the Earth as part of their Karmic cycle. Contrary to popular belief, the answer is simply "No". I will explain my answer.

Let us look at the cellular frequency of memory. Within the body lies a structure of energy pertaining to the cell structure, which allows you to replace all cells in order that growth can manifest. However, not only within the cellular structure is there the life force of creation to enable you to grow and replenish and re-energise, but there is a core factor of memory. Within every cell, there is a core factor of memory.

It is the imprint deity of every action that you have made. Every thought, all memory, is encoded within every cell. That is why one looks at cycles of sickness, and within cycles of sickness, it is re-activated by thought and memory in relationship to the coding of this Planet with the alignment of various Star Systems, which are magnetic. In other words, like a giant poultice drawing up memory from various parts of ones body and re-activating on another level the memory factor of fear.

Within the genetic coding lies a structure of possibilities, and as you incorporate a directive flow of life activating the genetic coding as such when you take on form upon this Planet, you take on a Blueprint also which is composed of structure weaknesses and strengths of that particular line of genetics.

Those genetic values are held in abeyance until it is deemed necessary to release various memory particles which are encoded. This is with the understanding before life was taken on in a bodily form that the weaknesses within the genetic coding could be activated by memory.

For example, the blueprint of Cancer and other diseases are ready to be activated if the thought of fear allows it, but it does not have to do that. Please listen to that. You do not have to have disease, even if it is encoded within with a great genetic possibility, you can by-pass the fear aspect of that coding.

Let us just imagine for a moment that you have before you someone who is suffering and in pain. Their body is not vibrating to the energy of their desire, and so they are not in harmony within the meridians of their energy. So you lay your hands upon them, and you ask that the light and love manifest into their Being to release their suffering.

The person feels the energy vibrate through their body, through the power of your thought and also through the power of theirs, wanting to be healed, Therefore, a slight change may occur, but nothing was healed. Only the thought was healed temporarily.

The illusion of the mind within healing is a powerful tool. When you touch another, you re-arrange the vibration rate according to the power point of your delivery, which is your thought. I wonder how many people would know that. One does not realise the power of ones thought.

You need to know that you take on the responsibility of the re-arrangement of energy when you attach yourself to the frequency of healing. You cannot come into another's energy field and manufacture your own energy into theirs without them first accepting the possibility of that exchange, and how that may affect them.

Unfortunately, there are too many people believing how "great they are", interfering with the magnetic stream of reference of light, not caring at all for how the person feels, only for their own sense of duty of needing to create a viable component of delivery of healing. So that the other person will be better, to allow their image to be acceptable to many. How wrong that is and how wide-spread and prevalent it has become.

What is true healing you ask? It is when the power of light enters within the core of your Being. That is true healing. It is when the mind encounters itself in disarray. When the power of light emanates within every cellular component of its Being, and it remembers. It remembers that it is not in alignment with its Creator. Only then healing is complete.

Let us look at the one who calls themselves a "healer". Within the energy field of the healer lies a great assortment of viable frequencies that may or may not be ignited through the power of thought, which is called "caring".

How can darkness instigate light? How can confusion instigate harmony in another? How can fear instigate no-fear? It is not possible. They are playing games, and they call it "healing". So let us get "real", and look at allowing the greater part of "what" you are to manifest, and through no expectation, just an acknowledgement of the creative frequency of light, one touches another, and together you manifest a reaction. A reaction within the remembering of "what" you are.

One being the conductor and one being the receiver. Only then can true healing take place. Not through befuddled minds and through egotistical references of self-importance. Nothing at all is done, except to make another expect to be well, that is all.

You wish to make another well. You wish to heal them. Perhaps they do not really want to be well. Had you thought of that? If one wants to stay in the darkness of doubt and fear, and their physical body reacts, well let them stay there. That is their choice.

However, if they put out their hand to you and ask you to assist them, then that is different, but do not go to their corner of darkness and get out all of your healing tools or whatever you have, or put your hands upon them to balance their energies, that is no good to anyone.

You are to look at them in their corner and say, "Have a nice time there, enjoy your misery, because you have created it, and perhaps you want to stay there because it is safe, and that is alright. I can only help you when you recognise where you are, and that you do not want to stay there." Only then can change happen.

So many people are magnetised to the service of healing. We need to look at the illusion of service. Mankind operates on the misconception that he needs to be of service to another. He looks for an avenue of service to which he can become his "Brothers Keeper". You may argue this point admirably, that each one needs a caretaker to instigate an energy reactor system of love.

However, we wish to say unto you that the reactor of love is a farce. It is incorporated within your corporate world of magnificence of trying to find the evaluation of light. Light cannot be evaluated, it can only be known.

Healing seems to be so "in", and you can feel very important with being "in". You fragment other's energies by allowing the infiltration of your illusion of services to manifest an answer to the human ailments.

I need to make my point very clear, and no doubt it will not be accepted by many, but no matter. A fact is a fact. You do not have the power to heal. You provide the energy to assist the possibility of a balance within the frequency field of thought. That is what you do.

When the power structure of a few individuals upon your Planet use the Greater Essence of the Divine Plan, they are the "instruments" of a greater power beyond your comprehension, and that "tag" is not given too lightly to many. They do not call themselves "healers" as such, but "messengers of light".

Healing is done through the power structure of light that infiltrates thought, but not thought alone. By that I mean not a singular conscious thought, but the thought which is the original thought of light.

Many have been used as examples to show the power of light, and took on a physical disability in order to show others what was possible when one incorporated beyond the thought mechanism of self. Unless the power of thought through the self is changed, healing cannot be activated.

You have asked a question relating to the span of life and if the time frame of your life was predetermined before you entered life upon Earth.

To use your point of reference, if you are an "Earthling", and are not en-coded beyond the frequency of this Planet, it is usually a set structure. If however, you are a Reflection from a greater dimension, it is open-ended.

Let us look at the "open-ended" example, and let us use the scenario of someone who looks after their physical body in accordance to the current condition of its genetic frame, acknowledging perhaps that there is a particular organ that is a little weaker than another. They therefore regulate that organ with the power of light, holding off its incompleteness, its imperfection.

Therefore, and listen to this, it is dependent upon the higher range value which is called your "Higher Being", that makes the decision. The self regulates according to the Program of the Planet, which is survival.

The understanding on a higher level by-passes the coding of thought and memory here upon this Planet and allows the frequency to be available to blend harmoniously with the power that it is when it recognises that it has completed the codings that are necessary. Remembering that the codings can also be drawn upon on other levels.

You ask about self-proclaimed "holy people" who claim that they can "heal" many and also "raise the dead". Whenever you see the result of light, you see the result of love. The message of light does not instigate an energy that needs to fulfil itself with adoration and power.

Those to whom I work with, work diligently and quietly with no titles, just the frequency of the delivery of light, to dark places of where light has been forgotten. There is no power in that. There is no name in that.

Mankind should not bow in homage to another, but instead should bow homage to that "what" he is. There is no separation between one who is seen as greater or lesser. For all is the same, just vibrating differently, to a different note. All come from the "Fathers House", and all will return. All is light. All is perfect.

If one finds that they have comfort in another's viewpoint, or promises or delivery or whatever, then allow them that. It may not be of comfort to you, but to them it is. They still recognise the separation value and they are entitled to that.

Do not blame those who stand up and perform tricks, for they are but an example beyond the frequency of illusion, by creating illusion.

The illusion is not within the tricks, but within the minds of man. The illusion is separateness, to look up to another who can create many things, is to not allow the power of their own making to manifest. They are too busy looking outwardly, and how can they register their inward motion of life if their gaze is on an outward connection.

Let me give to you an example. If I love you totally, and I am so engrossed in my love for you, it follows me everywhere, and my devotion would be so great that all else does not exist except the power of my love and devotion. All my energy has been placed within that. How can I see that what I am when I am looking at you all of the time?

I have given to you a generalisation of healing, and through this generalisation, I hope that you will see the main factors. You cannot heal anyone. All you can do is be the viable conductor of light, and the other person is the viable receiver of light. It cannot work unless both of you are in agreement with this.

I have been a little controversial with the subject of "healing", and have gone completely against the mainstream of thought that so many rely upon. However, perhaps it is time that mankind released his image of what "healing" is, in order that the reality of "healing" can be understood.

Chapter 13

The Return Journey

The imagery of time has to be understood through the reality of the "now". You speak of a "Return Journey", but there is no Journey, it is the relationship to the movement of awareness. That is what is echoing out into all areas of your lives.

When you relate to the energy of the return, it is the return of the original knowing. Not the movement through time, but time itself is an indicator of a connection to movement and memory. It is the uncovering of the reality of the knowing that is called, through your image, "The Return Journey of Remembrance."

There is no sound, no echo, just the silence where no words, no movement enters into. It is just the knowing, the totalness of all without any form, without any sound, any movement.

It is the relationship of the totality to itself. The Journey forward and backward is only the image reflector, given so that you can by-pass and fragment all memory within the energy structure of your illusionary reality, at any given point.

We justify this by asking you, "At this moment in your time, where does your reality come from?"

Does it come from the investigation of the "no- love?" The "no-love" is the indicator of your reality of your movement through your current lifetime. That will be concurrent, I repeat, concurrent with various other frequencies that co-exist within your reality through your illusionary Time Frame.

The Return Journey through the imagery to which you are relating, has to join all frequencies through the 7 Light Bodies of awareness, and the 7 levels of the Inner Being through the Inner Worlds.

All has to be joined together once again with no imagery. All frequencies are of the same note. They are each a by-product of the other through whatever reality and Time Frame you are currently exposed to, with your consciousness.

Your question should be - "What is the Journey?" Are you currently upon it? Are you currently awakening to the Remembrance, or are you just on an illusionary, with the term of phrase, "revolutionary uncovering?" The answer to this is three-fold.

1. You are totally aware at all times of your light. That is the indicator of all movement.
2. You are encased within a Time Frame of the consciousness of this lifetime, however illusionary to you.
3. You are co-existing with a greater part of yourself, which is beyond the Program of this Planet. It is greater than you can ever imagine.

All three connect in order that you can manifest a movement within your consciousness, within your Time Frame, within the greater power of "who" you are. So that all can be revealed through the "no-love" of this Planet, and incorporated through and into the Greater Mind, so that all can co-exist together through the memory of all existence.

You speak of the memory of your Planet as being "the" memory, and yet the Greater Mind is the main memory that all eventually relate to. Your light, the reality of your light, is only known because of the memory of the Greater Mind.

You ask the question "Is the transmutation, that is needed to be undergone upon Planet Earth, from the memory that you have created there?"

I will answer - The weakness of human character is to co-exist within their memory of what they wish they could be. They do not wish to be light, so they do not create it, but light does not have form, and therefore cannot be manipulated.

The Planet Earth is the manipulator of form and imagery. To transmute that, one has to acknowledge that form has no value, and it is in the "Return Journey of Remembrance" that formless becomes the apparent victor. What form really is, is the creative genius of mankind's imagery of control and power, so that he can separate and keep creating separation, in order that there is more form to control.

Transmutation is only, listen to this, is only the realisation that form is illusion, and that light is all there ever has been, and light does not need to create anything. "No-love" is fear. Fear to reveal that form has no power.

Form is the creator of mankind's imagery of greatness to manipulate matter into a "co-creator" of illusion so that it can bring about the complete separation value by divisional thought and memory.

Also, by being only aware of mankind's own sound in order that he does not have to release himself back into the reality where there is no power, no thought, no memory, no form. "No-love" is fear. Fear of losing separateness.

Is matter what thought created? Or is matter even creation itself? Matter is a by-product of creative thought. Creative thought through the dimension of the sound, the note, that the Earth relates to.

All other planetary frequencies have a similar sound. Matter does not exist when you are not the same sound. When you do not relate to that sound, that note, then matter does not exist. It is only existing upon one note, one frequency, so that all can be held together to create the solid form that you call matter.

Once the note does not resonate to incorporate physical well-being, then the physical shell of matter ceases to operate because the light has been withdrawn. No longer needed to operate upon that note.

Your question should be - "Is mankind a servant to matter? Or does he create matter to be his servant?" An interesting question for you to work with.

Chapter 14

Reincarnation

Let us look at the misunderstood subject of "Reincarnation." What if I told you that your memories of previous lives, may not in fact belong to you?

With that statement, comes a need to place new reference to the image of what one calls "Reincarnation". Many religions and doctrines encompass the actuality and possibility of living more than one life in order to pay "penance" for what has been done in previous lives. However, I wish to say unto you this day, that the subject of "Reincarnation" bears a greater insight into evolution than has previously been acknowledged.

Within the dominion of light, there exists the reaction of needing to cover countless possibilities through the evolutionary process. This is done through Aspects and Fragments.

The Aspects being the main "light bearers" and the Fragments being the "off-shoot" sparks of light that are required to exist within a Time Frame of existence, in order that the evolutionary cycle can be fulfilled.

To put it simply, means that, there are seven dimensions within your Universe. The Aspect resides upon the highest frequency or note of its attainment through its evolutionary cycle.

Upon the lower frequency dimensions, resides Fragments of its light that have taken on "form" in order to fulfil the obligation of "Reincarnation". This is so that all memory of its encounter with life can be transferred back to the Aspect, which, in turn, retains all memory and experience upon the Higher Mind level of its Being.

Whilst the Aspect remains, for example, within this Universe, it has upon each dimension fragments of its light, encountering individuality within form.

When the "Shift" occurs, the Aspect retracts all Fragments from all dimensions back into itself. All memory intact from all possibilities and experiences covered by the Fragments through the evolutionary cycle of life upon these dimensions.

The Aspect has therefore released the need to have the Fragments upon all dimensions of that Universal scale. Thereby retracting them, so that the "thrust" through the higher coding system can then allow the Aspect to move into the next Universe. It will then occupy the lowest note of that Universal scale. Once again, fragmenting its light in order that the evolutionary awakening can occur through a new range of possibilities and experiences.

However, upon Planet Earth at this point in time, are many who have come from beyond this Universe, and who come from other Star Systems in the form of "reflections" of a major Aspect. I speak of "reflections" and not "fragments" of light.

You may ask, "What is the difference between Reflections and Fragments?" Fragmentation means it is not of the same value as what it originally was. A Reflection is a division of itself within a lower note or frequency of acknowledgement, still being of the same value, but only able to exist within a limited sense within the frequency of its existence.

Back to my original statement. Your memories of your previous lives may not belong to you. You are "Reflections" from a greater part of what you are, occupying a physical vehicle upon this Planet Earth. There are many, many others who are also "Reflections" from beyond this Planet, but have not as yet awakened to the fact that this is so.

Within the Reflection that you are, is a coding of light that allows for the re-connection of that "what" you are to be viable through the "self". The "self" being the creator of illusion within your life.

The Brothers of Light have descended down into this lower Universal realm through a coding evaluation system that allows them to register an imprint upon this Lower Universe. I will not go into the complex coding system at this point, but instead I need to impart that the new Light Patterns from the New Program within the "Shift" will allow many, for the first time, to awaken up to that "what" they are.

When you look at memories, you look at your conditioned life within this Planet through the "self". That is all that you do. Beyond this connection, lies a more advance stream of memory, which, is in fact, the memory of "where" you really reside.

As I stated before, it is beyond this Universe, and your yearning to "go home" as you look upward into your skies at night, issues forth a directive to the consciousness that you do not belong here, upon Planet Earth.

You are occupying form within a physical vehicle that has inherited, listen to that, inherited memories from a "Fragment" that resides within the "Spirit World" of this Planet. This statement may throw you into complete confusion. I would expect that it would. I can almost hear your brain trying to fit it in with your current "misconception" of what "Reincarnation" previously meant to you.

Do not use your brain! It does not know. If it did, then no surprise will be registered. If that is the case, then good. You are on the right track of remembering.

Let us take it slowly, so that your brain does not go on "over-load" and completely switch off to what I am saying. Let us firstly look at the fact of you being a "Reflection", as so many are, upon Planet Earth. Within the "Reflection" that you are, is encoded memories.

These memories are three-fold. They are memories that your brain understands as being of your current life. You also have within you, memories that have been transferred into the cellular memory bank of your physical vehicle from a "Fragment" within the "Spirit World" of this Planet. Then you have the memory of that "what" you are, which is the memory of where you really are upon the evolutionary journey "back home" to the Absolute.

As you sit horrified, some of you, thinking that you are a duplicate of a Fragment, then I must put your mind to rest. We have taken from the Spirit World an empty "energy shell" that is no longer required by the Aspect.

We have thereby used this "energy shell" and have re-connected to its Aspect in order to draw from the memory of that Aspect all that was needed to impart a memory coding for your existence upon this Planet. We have only taken an imprint of memory from the Aspect, and have not disturbed in any way the fuller value of memory within the Aspect.

You must understand that this is done in order for you to believe that you are, in fact, fully connected to the memory of this Planet. The data of memory contains useful information that will assist you in your life. However, within this memory bank will also be, what you would term, "negative memories". These "negative memories" will, in fact, allow you to draw from the strength of your Inner Light, in order to transmute the energy within the memories.

This will show you the power that you have available. Thus awakening you up to the realisation of that "what" you are. We call it "stringent testing procedures". We can assure you that the power that you are could very easily over-ride any fear within any memory that you have inherited.

What we have also done is to place a coding regulator within your Being, so that you can awaken and re-connect back to "what" you are through the "frequency dimensional units" when the higher energies from the Brothers of Light descend upon this Planet. This allows for the awakening process to occur, firstly through the night state in your sleeping hours.

You could call your sleeping time your awakening time. In reverse. This will then, in turn, transfer a need to make complete change in your life, and many will feel fear because they have to let go of all that which they have held near and dear to them for so long.

Many will pull back with anger and unsureness. Their brains will work overtime at trying to dismiss what they are feeling, and they will not understand their conflict. For others, the "duality" is born. Duality meaning that they remember that "what" they are whilst still acknowledging through the self the connection to all they have created whilst upon this Earth.

As the higher coding systems start to operate via the Galactic Command, the connection to memories that were encoded from the Aspect via the Fragment will be obliterated. All that will be left within the memory bank will be the memory of your current lifetime, and the memory of that "what" you are.

Your question may be - "Why do I need to be here upon this Planet Earth as a Reflection? What is my purpose here?" If this was your question, then you have not as yet awakened up to that "what" you are or else you would know.

So to those to have not as yet fully awakened, I wish to speak to you. You are here so that the power of your light can register within the darkness of the illusion of this Planet. This Planet that has for so long been encased with thought and memory within fear.

Your power of light will bring a reaction through the negative frequency within the collective consciousness of Earth into a new cycle of light.

Thus allowing the "Shift" to be able to be experienced by all those who previously had not been able to let go of their fear. This will allow all Aspects within this Universe to reclaim that what belongs to them.

As the new Light Patterns from the "Fathers House" connect to Earth, all will be transmuted into a higher frequency of light. What we need you all to do is to let go of all that you think you are, and that may be so difficult for many of you.

Allow the memory of our great love for you to carry you through your fear. To let go of all beliefs and doctrines that your conditioning has attached to you, and "remember". Remember that you are more than you think you are. The power of your light has always been available to you.

Do not let the self be your power, Let the remembering of that "what" you are to manifest through your image of what you believe your life to be. Release yourselves from your doubt, your fear. You cannot see your light when you do not allow yourselves to remember.

Upon this Planet there will be a revolution, A revolution of light. There is change all around you, but it is not enough. For change within many is so temporary, for the self always dictates the conditions of life. Do not create any more illusion. For goodness sake! Do not create anything.

Let the magnetic law of your light do the work. The magnetic law is perfect. For as your remembering takes place, your light will draw to it all that which it needs, so that your purpose upon this Planet can finally be fulfilled.

You are all so loved. Remember that.

Chapter 15

Aspects and Fragments

We will now look at the most important issue of Aspects and Fragments. First of all, however, we must point out that all are on their way back "home" to the Fathers House.

There is no greater or lesser, for all is within the movement of the illusion that all is separate.

Within the separation factor that creates what you would call individuality, there is a rather interesting example for us to reveal unto you. This is the procedure of confirming within your limited appraisal that all are "reflections of the light".

These "reflections" have taken on form through the process of existing within a Time Frame, or what you would call an awareness cycle, within the Universal relationship to the concept of evolution.

These reflections, therefore, take on the energy by-product of that Universal frame of existence, thereby creating Aspects and Fragments.

Aspects being the main light bearer within the relationship factor to that Universe, and the Fragments being the by-product evaluation system, which allows for multiple possibilities to be explored through the evolutionary cycle within the Time Frame of existence.

For example, within the Universe that you currently occupy, there are a vast array of "notes" or "frequencies" to be connected to. The Earth is upon the lower range of "notes" within this Universal spectrum.

Through ages past in your time evaluation, there are many who have gone beyond the Planet Earth, but have not gone beyond the Universe that the Earth occupies.

When we speak of the "Shift", this allows those upon the highest note of that Universe to shift into the next Universe, thereby taking the next major step upon their journey home.

Upon your Planet Earth is a great residue of energy that is the resultant factor of fragmentation energy. Many, many Fragments exist upon Planet Earth. They are re-cycled by the Aspects, who in fact have gone on beyond this Planet to connect to a higher range of notes upon other Planetary existences. I would expect you to ask, "But why did they not transmute their Fragments before they went on to encounter a new dimension of understanding?" This is a question that needs to be asked, and indeed needs to be answered.

The Aspect upon a Universal level needs to incorporate the complete range of notes within the scale of that Universe. Let us use an analogy within a simple way.

Let us look at a Piano. Let us look at the Piano as being a composite of differing scales of notes. Each scale of notes occupies a diverse range of possibilities within the sound that the notes make. The Earth is upon the left-hand side of the Piano, and we will call this the first scale of notes.

When each scale of notes is mastered, it can be registered as a "sound", thereby all notes vibrating together. All is registered within that scale. There are, in fact, seven scales within your Universe. Thus being seven sounds.

When all sounds resonate together, that is called a "Program". All notes within that Universe have been registered and recorded by the Aspect. All is known upon that level of existence. Evolution within that Universe has been fulfilled, thus allowing the Aspect to connect to the next Universe.

The Aspect needs to still recognise the "sound" of the Planet Earth, or else all notes would not make a complete sound within the Program of that Universe. Therefore, Fragments are left upon each Planetary note, until the time of the next Universal "Shift" takes place. Which, as you know, is very soon.

Upon the end of a Universal cycle that precedes the "Shift", the Aspect returns to the lowest end of the Piano to gather up all that which has been left behind. The Aspect cannot connect with the next Universe until all Fragments have been transmuted back into the Light that it is.

You might ask, "Has the Aspect left any Fragments upon the other Planetary scales of reference?" My answer is no. I simply say to you that the Aspect has drawn all Fragments through the Time variation through what you would call the "future."

Hence the future has come back into the past. The past being the Planet Earth. All else has been transmuted. The Earth being the lowest scale that has to be transmuted.

Within the reflection that you are, you will have to understand that the reflection is only accorded this title because it is not a complete unit of light. When we say "not complete" we mean that there is an absence of the reality frequency of light that resides within the Fathers House.

We use the terminology "Fathers House" because we need to instil a reactionary vocabulary within you to understand that there is a more far reaching awakening to come. Within the reflection there is only an echo of a sound, a shadow of light, but it is not the fullest realisation of that what it is.

The Universal scales of reflections have allowed all to flow through the evolutionary cycle of discovery through varying frequencies that assist in the recognition of what life and light actually mean.

Life is, in fact, the evolutionary term that allows individuality to exist within the energy structure of that Planet, and within the Time Frame of existence of what is needed in order for an evaluation through thought/memory/time to be encountered.

Through life, the Aspect is able to relate to many diverse and responsive issues that show to it the illusion of existence.

Through the fragmentation process, it develops an awareness through countless options and opportunities that are directly related to the magnetic frequency that it issues forth.

The Fragments are in fact "held up" within a Time Frame for the reason mentioned before. That is to allow the Aspect to exist within another dimension of consciousness, within another dimension of light, within another dimension of knowing, whilst the discovery of that "what" it is allows the Aspect to be retracted through the magnetic law of compliance, which you call "karma". The Fragments are held within "the past" upon the Planet that is necessary for its survival.

All experiences that the Fragments have are transferred through the Higher Light Coding Patterns that are centred within the Universe of where all reside. Through these Coding Regulators, the Aspect receives all relevant "sounds" from other scales of that Universe, in order for it to have a complete recognition of all energy "data".

Whilst this sounds quite complex, within its complexity there is a simplicity. Through your brain, that has no reference, there is an enquiry that allows confusion to reign. When one has no registration within the brain, it becomes difficult to fully understand what is meant.

However, if you would just allow the simple example that all is one, and that an Aspect is a light that allows beams of its light to explore the illusion of darkness, then perhaps you will finally understand that the illusion of separation allows evolution to be the uncovering of what is already known, but long forgotten.

Through systematic shifts of awareness, all will return back to where they reside, and that is within the Fathers House. When you look, really look with the knowing that you have, you will finally see that all that is within life is light. That is all.

When you really know that you are light, life ceases to have a need to hold onto you. You have been drawn back within the power of "what" you are. It is all so simple, yet for many it will be all so complex.

Chapter 16

Duality

Within your Being is a light. That light cannot be viewed when you are not looking within your Being, I ask, "Where is your vision?" Does your vision encompass that to which you have inherited, and that is the light that you are, or do you not use the advantage of your physical well being to look beyond the capability of what you can.

Many are well rehearsed with the energy of life. I wonder if you are as well rehearsed with the energy of light. There is a marked difference. Yet you only view life and not light. You are like embryos within the frequency division of knowing and not-knowing.

You try to regulate through your beliefs that to which you should inherit, and that is the "all knowing" through belief structures and visual capacity, and allowing your ears to hear the words of wisdom from those who call themselves wise.

There is great confusion upon your Planet. There are those who call themselves "wise" and know nothing, and those who say they know nothing, and have the makings of being wise.

I wonder where you are listening from? Is it through your inherited belief structure that you have the capacity of "all knowing" whilst in the physical counterpart of your expression on this Earth?

I wish to say unto you that, whilst you occupy physical form, you will never be wise, because all you have is a frequency division within form that has nothing to do with light. It is only life that you are working with, and not light, and as you are wondering to what I am speaking of, I will reiterate more simply.

Within the brain that you have, are components of memory, You know of this, and yet I do not believe that you register the complete acknowledgement of the power of that memory. Your life not your light, is the major division from knowing and not-knowing.

You are a complexity in form of wanting to surrender back to "what" you are, and yet trying so hard to stay with "who" you are. Whilst this display of possibilities goes nowhere, you become lost once again upon the stream of life.

Within the knowledge aspect of your delivery within your memory, you resonate very loudly. Your past incarnations have heralded a complete exact duplicate of your present understanding and by that we say, "You have not even started to bypass the energy of your memory if you are only resonating within knowledge and not knowing." What is "knowing" you might ask. Is that different, or is that just another aspect of knowledge? Knowledge is the gateway to illusion. That is a fact. Knowledge will lead you everywhere but back to "what" you are. It is a duplicate bypass system for illusion to be maintained.

What is knowledge? Is it a complete picture that lies before you that gives to you a greater insight into what "light" is? Or is it, in fact, a diagram that resembles a maze, a maze of conflict with no way out because you have not created one.

Your Planet Earth resonates to the complexity of memory within knowledge. Knowledge being the forefather that one calls "wisdom." We call "stupidity".

Yet you say, "We have knowledge," and I say unto you, and listen carefully each one, "Allow knowledge only to stay for a short while, whilst you acknowledge also within knowledge the "Absolute" frequency of light, and not the delivery of experience through life."

You are more than you think you are, and yet you have pain in your hearts. You do not understand joy. You have unsureness, and you have pride, and within the elemental faction of your fear, lies the self.

I wish to speak, not to the self this evening, for it knows not what I speak of, but to that "what" you are. May you hear the words, so that you can resonate once more beyond the image that has been created by the self.

When we speak of a "re-connection", perhaps you do not quite understand what a connection means. It is not connected through your memory or your brain, but rather through the duplicate system of energy that vibrates to a greater frequency than what you currently believe. Some of you are in duplicate, and some of you are in triplicity.

The power that you are, you have not even touched it yet, and how you smile smugly, some of you, with the satisfaction of life, and how foolish that is. If you wish to smile with the satisfaction of your creation of life, then so be it, but there is more.

You have the advantage of living within a Time Frame of releasing that which is not to the energy faction of what your duplicate system resembles. "He speaks in a complicated way," I hear you say.

Let us look at "who" you are, and then let us look at "what" you are. Some of you do not even acknowledge "who" you are, so how could you expect to acknowledge "what" you are. Within the energy of "who" you are lies complex mechanism of thought and memory, that vibrates to a greater memory bank within your Being.

I wish you to acknowledge that through the self in this moment in your time, you are resonating and relating to current conditions through the structure of your requirements at this point in time. However, that is not necessarily the component of energy of memory of "who" you really are, because on the morrow you will react differently. I hope you are following me.

So when you say that you know who you are, you only know who you are today, but you do not know who you will be tomorrow. So you say, "Yes, I know who I am, and so now I can work at re-connecting back to "what" I am." Then I say unto you, "Stop! Leave alone the "who" you are, and let us look at "what" you are".

The "what" you are is stable, It is an energy frequency of light, not life, that is being expanded and translated from another frequency in time altogether.

I say this to you, all of you, without exception. "There is none here in this room resonating only to the Earthly evolution." That is a fact, So I speak to my fellow Brothers of Light of "what" you are, Hear my words, and remember.

The power of your light can be seen, but in some it is only flickering, but you will remember that the light that you are is based upon the power of the Major Aspect that allows the energy of your light to be transmitted from where you are. I do not wish to sound complex, I just wish you to remember that you are being re-connected, whether your self likes it or not, Whatever power you wish to use will be regulated firstly by the self, but you have to acknowledge the limitedness of frequency of light that is available.

Forget your petty ways, I speak now to the self. Forget your foolishness in trying to discover truth. It does not exist. It is only an imagery of what you believe it to be. Instead acknowledge finally, and let go, because the final stages of light descending from the "Fathers House" is nearly upon you.

Release unto "what" you are the power, so that the "what" can regulate it and not allow the self to be the complete victor.

You are a duality within the energy of "who" and "what" you are, but the triplicity goes even further. That is "who" you are, "what" you are, and the possibility of re-connecting to a greater example of light from the main frequency centre from the 5th Universal Frame. That is not for many, so do not get too excited.

So let us look at your limitedness and your fear, and your indecisiveness and your ego, and let us bundle them up and throw them away, for they have no use to you anymore. Show me "what" you are so that you can see me. So that you can hear me. So that I can love you.

Allow my energy to help you to remember. Let us share together the light that each one is, so that this Planet can start to understand that there is no division, there is no hatred, there is no fear, there is only the joy of discovery of light.

How you cry each one, as you wrestle with your fears, and how you bow your head and you wonder, "What can I do so that my life can be better?" The answer is simple. Allow the light to do the work instead of your created life.

Chapter 17

The Shift

Let us talk about the "Shift." If you look at the Planet Earth through your current observation, you will see the ending of many cycles of thought.

The circumference of your Earth is now being endowed with new light. The basis of the "Shift" is relegated to "Light". A new Light Pattern that is emanating from the "Absolute Light" which we call the "Fathers House".

Thought, which has played its part in the creative imbalance of many, has relegated to itself an uncovering of fear. Within fear is memory, and memory re-activates fear.

Within the current cycle of your Planet Earth, one has to instigate an awakening. For within the polarity of its nucleus, it reaches out beyond its dominion, whereby its light is no longer able to sustain the energy of deliverance of that which mankind requires to fulfil the destiny of evolution.

To place it in your terms of reference, the Earth is to shift into a new cycle of light. From the Higher Heavens new Light Patterns are emerging, and all through the many varying levels and dimensions of this Universe, all is being incorporated into the finer essence of light.

To draw from this light is what seems so difficult for so many, when one is so used to the darkness of self, which has within it its own creative thought patterns from memory.

Whilst light has never gone anywhere, one has to incorporate new dimensions of thinking that opens up the greater expectation of deliverance of what God is to them.

While many wrestle with their memories to try to keep them under control, they are, in fact, endowing them with re-created thoughts and opinions through memory, Many are looking for their salvation through the uncovering of many events that dictate the closing of one Time Frame in order to open another.

If you look at "Revelations" within your Bible, they are also inherent in many religious doctrines throughout your world, in varying forms and idealistic observations, as to how one looks at them. For within the creative genius of ones mind, you will find an observation of "God."

Each one has their own nucleus of observation through their current Time Frame of reference, and so your Planet Earth is opening the doorway finally to the new acceptance of light.

The light that has been forsaken for so many, in terms of thousands of years, has always been available, but has not been drawn upon because the Earth itself has not allowed it to be so.

The cycle to which your Moon is operating on, is relevant to the uncovering of the masking of many. The inner doctrines that clothed your Inner Temples of ages past, are bringing about the resurrection of old thought patterns that many are clamouring to incorporate into their knowledge.

When one looks at the pattern of observation, of where one is or is not, it is through the finite mind and not through the greater observation of all. The mind is patterned with many particles of light. Each one existing solely into the reflection of what really is being forwarded. It is like having, in your terms, a "dirty mirror", but in certain places it is able to incorporate the reflection.

That is how we see your Earth. There are pockets of light allowing a fuller reflection to come in, Through the darkness of doubt and fear the Planet is now absorbing light through the "stations" that we have placed upon the planet. There is an opening up through the measurement that you will make of a frequency, so that the light can become even stronger.

Many will flinch through their old Program, and will not understand as to why they cannot incorporate the awareness and awakening that many are talking about.

The Light Vehicles upon the Planet will become even more enhanced by the energy that is being forwarded through the "Galactic Command", who serve as a reservoir of the "Father's" power.

Through the sub-stations within the dimensions of your lower four frequency levels, you will find that they are working hard to frequent the Planet with many varying energy points, in order that many will uncover the direction that they have already discussed through the "Great Ones" connection.

So, you can look at a ball of rock within an endless sky as being a third dimensional problem. A problem that will cease. All will cease to be in conflict, for as the light penetrates in its full value of being, the magnetic points on the Planet will shift, and the energy of the Earth will be lifted through the change of magnetic shift.

As the magnetic shift changes through the Light Patterns, it will connect to the Light Pattern of one's own Being, and will be drawn up into the fullness of the new Program.

That is all I have to say regarding the "Shift."

Chapter 18

Programming

I need to tell you this. Through the illusion of separation from that "what" you are, comes an image of light. That light is the exact duplicate within non-reality, that needs to connect back to itself, which we will call "reality".

Within that re-connection process evaluation is evolution. Evolution quite simply works through adopting back light into the illusion of itself in order to "go home".

When we say "go home", we mean that all needs to bypass the Space and Time Frame of its existence in order to incorporate a new dimension of awareness. This is done through light streams, also known as a "Program."

This Program contains a coding system that allows the illusion of where you believe yourself to be to allow you to "shift" into another phase of your awakening process.

For example, the Earth upon which you live has been encoded with a Program of Light. This light is an energy formation that comes from the "Fathers House." Evolution is within a framework of cycles. I want you to remember that all is magnetic, in that all has to return back from whence it came. This is done in accordance to cycles of frequency patterns of light, known as the "Program" of that point in reference within that Time and Space Frame.

The Earth has reached the end of its current Program or Light Pattern frequency. Therefore, it will be transmuted by a new Program that is sent from the "Fathers House" to allow it to continue within a new awareness existence, until it is deemed that the Earth has fulfilled its function in the evolutionary process within the Time/Space frequency that it occupies.

There are multiple coding systems to each Program, and I will speak of this more fully at a later time. However, for the moment, we need you to recognise that the magnetic value through the coding system allows all to "re-connect" through cycles of Light Programs that enable the note of awakening upon that level of awareness to be operational.

The self has its own coding system that operates by establishing a liaison through multiple lifetimes with the major coding component within the Planet Earth.

Each lifetime allows a multiple of light frequencies to formulate a coding system for that particular lifetime. As each lifetime is experienced, the major coding system of Planet Earth allows a new frequency of awareness through what one calls a "lesson" to be experienced. So it goes on, until all possibilities within the coding mechanism are experienced.

In order to fulfil the entitlement of transmuting the illusionary process of life through the awareness pattern of light, which is the coding, it is ascertained that many lifetimes would be needed to complete the cycle of evaluation. Hence the need to fragment the energy of that spark of light, which you call the "Spirit", into many parts of itself. That is what we call the "Soul." A group of Souls is now functional. A "Soul Group" allows all possibilities to be explored.

Within each Universe are coding patterns of light. All returns back to the Fathers House through each Program's magnetic frequency shift.

Chapter 19

The Reactor

Your question pertains to the "Reactor". What is the Reactor and from whence does it obtain its connection to the vehicle within the physical reflection known as the "self?" Let us look at the by-product of what the Reactor has relayed, and that simply is the "self". You, the product of the evaluation system known as individual identity.

The Reactor has within it a Program device known as the "Coding System Modulator". This is, in fact, the energy from where you are, or what you would term your "what." The fact of the matter is, that the Reactor is the umbilical cord from the term of reference of "what" you are to "who" you are within the physical dimension of the Planet Earth.

The by-pass system is, indeed, through the Regulator that comes from beyond the "what" you are to ensure the possibility of allowing new Patterns of Light to emerge, that can, in fact, be connected to, so as to allow the "Shift" to give its full capacity to rotate the compliance factor within the sphere of the greatest possible recognition of what that Light Pattern means.

The emergence of the Reactor has, in fact, enhanced your delivery mechanism throughout the ages past. For through the circumference of varying Time Frame analogies, comes the vast array of different Pattern and Coding systems.

In fact, you would be well rehearsed with diverse patterns of light that allow the coding mechanism to operate upon the level of your communication value. Which, indeed, is upon the Planet Earth.

The Reactor is the connecting rod from where you are to ensure that the "who" you are is able to always be in contact with the greater dimension of "what" it is.

Quite simply, the Regulator allows the finer particles of that frequency within the Dimensional Units to always be viable, thereby allowing the accessibility of all known, and listen to this, unknown components to be measured by by-passing the Reactor itself.

So, indeed, the Regulator is the most important component to relate to, whilst the Reactor is the frequency of that which has been accessible within the higher frame of evolution that you have attained.

Chapter 20

The Regulator

I wish to speak about the "Regulator." What is a Regulator? - you may ask. My answer is this - Within the energy centre of your Universe there is a vast array of Light Patterns. Within each pattern is a coding Regulator. This Regulator operates the value structure of light that is possible to be drawn upon.

Within each Light Pattern is a stream of reference of Light Modulators. These Modulators are the incoming reference system from beyond this Universe. They allow the frequency evaluation system to operate.

Nearer to the time of the "Shift" will come a new assortment of light frequencies that will enhance the Regulation system to operate within a new by-product evaluation scheme. When we speak of Regulation systems, we are bringing to your attention the frequency adjustment of the light that comes through the Modulators within the structure of light patterns, that are viable within the Shift, into a new dimension of light awakening.

To put it simply would not give to you the full advantage of acknowledgement through your own understanding, thereby bypassing the exact range of new Frequency Dividers that are to become inherent within your being.

The total adjustment has to be allowed to arrange the new light sensors to operate. This in turn, will allow for a new frequency to become viable in relationship to the new Regulator that will over-ride all existing Regulators from other Time Frames within the Universal structure that the Earth occupies, but also through the relevant Time Frames beyond that.

The complexity of what a Regulator is, overlooks the fact of what it represents. This representation of new Light Patterns is to be the foremost evaluation connection to the brain space that you occupy. Light cannot be measured as we have often stated, and so the brain will not comprehend the maximum effect through the visual and sensory capacity until the fullest, I repeat, the fullest value has been established within all levels of existence.

I trust that you are now more conversant with what a Regulator is.

Chapter 21

Frequency Dimensional Units

When we speak of Frequency Dimensional Units we are speaking of the "outer" value of energy that does not exist upon this Planet.

Within the physical body lies the factor of memory. Memory that is stored within the brain that allows for the function of the "self" to exist. However, within the cellular component of the physical body lies a greater storehouse of memory.

Memory has to be understood as being more that the brain indicates. Memory has within it a more far reaching example to enable one to encounter the entirety of that "what" one is, way beyond the image of what the human vehicle recognises.

When you understand that memory is within all cells within your Being, you will then start to understand the value of your thought. Your thought is the indicator of the reaction of memory. Memory being the conductor of thought.

Within the cellular structure of your Being lies an advance formula of coding patterns. These coding patterns contain the frequency of "Light" in order to instigate a "remembering" of that "what" you are beyond this Planet. Planet Earth being the environment that your physical vehicle is occupying in order to fulfil the purpose of its incarnation within that frequency.

These coding patterns are known as "Frequency Dimensional Units", and are inherent within the cellular memory banks of all those who have by- passed the evolutionary cycle of Planet Earth. These Frequency Dimensional Units allow the "reflections" from the Major Aspect to instigate a remembering of the purpose for life upon Earth.

Chapter 22

Time Frames

The finer dimensions of thought offer up a sequence of a reactionary movement of thought. The Time Frames that give you all so much confusion, are only a "reactionary assessment of awareness".

Each Program has within it 7 Frequency Chambers. Each one reacting to the other. Let us look at 7 Light Bodies. Each Light Body contains a Regulator, which is, in fact, a reactionary frequency adjudicator.

The Time Frames are coded, and each one is connected to the other. They are 7 dimensional responses within a frame of recognition of what light is or is not.

Time Frames are only, I repeat, only awareness centres of realisation regulated by codes. These codes are connected to a major energy grid of the Planet Earth. This regulates the 7 Light Bodies and determines their frequency relationship to their awakening to their reality.

Let us have an analogy, You are within a corridor and there are 7 doors. Each door represents an environment, an acknowledgement, or even an understanding of light.

The first door can only be entered by the door from the corridor. However, it has an inter- connecting door to Room 2, Room 2 has an inter-connecting door to Room 3, and so on, until you are within Room 7.

Where would you go then? I can hear you say, "Well, I would use the door out into the passage-way." Yes, but if you did, where would you go then? The point I am trying to make is, that all rooms are in relationship to each other.

Each room represents an area of investigation, a completing of what needs to be understood, until one needs to move onward and search for new things, and so on. However, when one reaches Room 7 and takes the door out to the corridor, like you would no doubt suggest, they are back where they started from. Within the "reality" of 7 segregated frequencies, when, in fact, the 7 doors are illusionary.

If I was in Room 7, I would acknowledge firstly that Room 7 was identical to Room 1. Nothing was different except my acknowledgement of it. Nothing was changed except my expectation that I had moved onto something new. I hope that you are following me.

Your Earth is composed of 7 light frequencies. Each one the same as the other, except for the uncovering that it is. When you speak of light, you speak of the imagery of it through thought, do you not? I speak of it through the frequency to where I am.

It is the same with Time Frames. It is not time as you know it, but a registration of awareness. Illusion is only the regulator of division of light.

Back to our analogy - If you are within Room 1, then you realise that there are possibilities that you have not even tried. You soon become bored with Room 1, completing the acknowledgement of what is there. An expectation as you walk through into Room 2 allows you to acknowledge what you expect to acknowledge, and so you go on acknowledging all that which you expect to find.

You expect to find all that which you need to uncover. Who said that you need to uncover anything within the imagery of your expectation? Who said the light had been turned off? Do not think, follow what I am saying with the energy of knowing. You have not missed anything because there is nothing to miss.

Whilst you are looking for something to uncover, you create an image of expectation of what is possibly could be. So you create an image of no-love so that you can fit it in and call it completion and love.

You are going the opposite way by expecting that you are no-love creating an opportunity to place love where love is not. However, that is the illusion. No-love does not exist except within the imagery of what you think you are not. You think you are not love, so no-love is created so that love can be placed within it.

You have woven the imagery of this journey through matter, expecting to uncover no-love. Replacing that to which you have created, which is the emptiness to replace the image of love. Whatever you are looking for you will find. When you do not look for anything, it finds you.

Room 7 is the image of Room 1. Time Frames are the imagery of "no-light", trying to acknowledge that it needs light. Take away the image is to take away the illusion, is to take away the awareness, because it is not required.

Awareness, what does that mean? What is the requirement to equal awareness? When one "IS", it does not need awareness, because that is a measurement of what is not the "IS."

You create the environment to register the "no-love" through the image of needing to have love. You register that you are not light, and so you are trying to uncover the light within the registration of "no-light". Trying to find what you have missed, so that you can make it become alright. Creating what is not alright to make yourselves satisfied to feel complete again.

You are within an illusionary frame of reference, which is a physical manifestation, but you are not really occupying that Space and Time at all. You are a Reflection, that is all. You will cease to be a Reflection and become encased within memory when you register an awareness of memory It is all in "reverse", is it not?

And so it is a registration of energy through a Reflection that is encompassing the imagery of time.

You are reflecting through a frequency of imagery, re-enacting through the memory which is compatible with the frequency of your cell modular of your human embodiment. Illusionary, but non-illusionary when thought occupies its space.

What we are attempting to do is to allow you the duality with the freedom of coming and going whenever you wish, and not necessarily locked into the reflection of illusion. You have the imprint of reaction from life within the Time and Space that you occupy. However illusionary to me, real to you.

You register that illusionary energy through reactionary frequencies that allow the manifestation of energy to stay within that vehicle of thought, and so the Time Frame which is the valuation of reactionary memory, allows the physical requirement to stay stationary within the embodiment of the Reflection that you are. You do not have to fully manifest the illusionary energy within the Time Frame that you occupy.

You can have the duality which is the complete freedom within your illusionary Time/Space.

Chapter 23

Light Bodies

Through the night, comes the frequency shift to allow oneself to re-model themselves. To re-model means to change the state. When one is awakened to another frequency, one has to incorporate a new "Light Body".

The physical body is connected to many Light Bodies. Seven in number. Each one being the covering of another. The physical body is the densest body that you have and relate to. It is the last body to find the full realisation of change.

Each Light Body is actually magnetic. Magnetic through each of the circumferences of the perspex outer lining. Each Light Body has encased within it a perspex outer lining that it sees through. This is to separate the illusionary frequency from the "reality" frequency, of the transition stage from one Light Body to another.

If you are looking at the magnetic levels of the outer perspex casing, it has to disintegrate, but is also attached to the next Light Body.

It actually transfers itself with that frequency until it completely shatters. So it takes you from one frequency to another, which then changes right through to the actual physical body. It changes for its need of that frequency completely. So the sleep state reinforces the value of energy that the body needs.

When this transference starts to take place, it means that the body is not quite sure of its requirements, so it shifts from a very deep sleep pattern to very light patterns, to readjust, so that the actual cell modular of memory incorporating the new frequency can be actually stabilized. Light Bodies actually allow the magnetic adjustment system to operate by regulating the amount of "light" that is necessary for the acknowledgement of the release of one frequency into another.

Upon your Planet is a dense evaluation system that you may call "truth". However, within the process of uncovering the fuller value of that "what" you are, the Light Bodies come together. Each Light Body, of which there are 7, magnetically draw back to themselves the frequency of one "sound". That sound is the indicator of their acknowledgement of their re-connection of that "what" they are.

Within the Programming procedure, the Light Bodies play the role of allowing only the necessary potency of "light" to be viable within the consciousness of the physical body, The physical vehicle is the densest body, which occupies the space and time of Planet Earth.

Beyond the scope of the Light Bodies comes a greater insight into the "Mind" of the relationship to all. The Light Bodies are the complex regulation system for the re-connection process to occur.

Chapter 24

The Rotation of Compliance

We wish to speak about the "Rotation of Compliance." You will have to look at the memory banks that are serving no justice, in that the re-regulation and de-regulation of memory is now finding its way into a more solid observation point within the grid that your personality has afforded itself.

You often hear us speak of "7 degrees West." This term is an inference of movement that you will have to look at as a magnetic quality that, in fact, makes an observance of relativity through current memory patterns. I repeat, current memory patterns of the vehicle of which you are using.

Rotation is, of course, bringing up again either singular or collective memory from the memory banks that you have inherited. The memory banks can be seen as a storehouse of re-evaluation of the cycle of reference of where you are actually deeming your reality to be at.

The rotation is the term of reference of bringing about, in equal quantity, that which it needs to acknowledge, and that which it needs to not acknowledge, by saying, "The personality does not require to acknowledge anything that is not comfortable with itself." Therefore, the rotation factor takes two varying cycles.

Imagine one moving in one direction, and one moving in another. When one locks into the other one with the fabrication of energy of reaction, it is where one is actually drawing their magnetic response from within the memory bank or grid frequency that each physical, I repeat, physical attribute has. Within the memory bank are magnetic points of reference.

Have you realised that within the memory bank grid system there are certain frequencies that are triggered by magnetic inferences of Time and Space. In other words, you can look at an astrological frequency at that point as being the main bearer that will connect to a memory, and it will suddenly be rejuvenated. That is the magnetic quality of drawing something out of the memory bank.

So we have what is called a "personal memory bank" that connects to the "greater memory bank" of this Planet. Then you have your own memory bank of your particle of light, known as "frequency dimensional units" that connects to the reality of where you really are.

There are light bearers that have magnetic points of reference within the memory bank of the Planet, and of the personality. You are looking at your own memory bank that seems to you, at times, to cause you dismay.

However, memory as it is readjusted through the magnetic quality of light and sound, allows that memory to manifest itself in order that transmutation can take place.

That is why within cycles of the Earth there are wars and there are no wars. There are discoveries and there are no discoveries. All is a movement of recollection, for all is a movement of being withdrawn from anything that is apparent that it is new.

The Earth at this time has its own "Rotation of Compliance", whereby all memory is starkly registered within the imprint that it is. So that it can move forward and readjust its cycle away from the memory bank that is the old Program.

When one moves from an old Program, one has to register the movement, or else there is no movement. Remember that!

You have to register the movement away from one Program to another, or else you will still register the memory, but the memory is only there to indicate the illusion of separateness. That is all you need to know.

Questions and Answers

The following pages contain Questions and Answers.

The varying topics were covered at different times at different places with different people.

The people who attended these "sessions" came from varying backgrounds. Some were quite conversant with what Elonias was speaking of, and others were at the session for the first time.

You will note that Elonias uses a rather complex explanation to some questions, whilst other questions are answered very simply.

Elonias always speaks to the level of understanding that the majority of the group has. Thereby he uses his ability to "turn around" a question to someone who has asked it, if he believes that they are close to "knowing" the answer themselves.

He always says that people should not "modify" or "justify" anything, and I believe that you will see what he means within his answers.

Many within the groups went away a little confused, whilst others felt that a "great load" had been lifted from them, as the power of Elonias' answers created a "knowing" within them, even if their brain did not register a full understanding.

As you read this next section of the Book, I hope that you will experience the power of his answers, along with the humour he delivers them with.

Chapter 25

Q&A - Love

(Q: I would like to ask a question about love. My life has not been happy. I seem to have a lot of problems in relationships. At times I get really upset because I feel that no-one loves me. What am I doing wrong?)

ELONIAS: Let us look at the power of love. Let us look at that. You believe there is no-one who loves you. I would like to ask you a question, "Do you know what love is?"

(A: I think so.)

ELONIAS: You think so. But do you "know" so? There is a difference. When you "know" what love is, there is no unsureness, there is no measurement, for love is "absolute".

For love, the reality of love, surpasses the image of what you think it could be. I wonder if your problem is with the identification of another's acceptance or non-acceptance of yourself. If this is the case, this is not love, but is an expectation of a behavioural pattern, that one calls love.

You speak of having difficulties in relationships. I wonder what you expect from those relationships. The image of love is the greatest barrier to the awareness of complete unconditional love. For when one looks to another for love so that they can feel "complete", this is an image that has been created so that you can feel "safe" and "wanted". But it is not love.

Mankind journeys through his life creating the environment so that he can experience the value of love. He uses his environment to its fullest, drawing material wealth, possessions and success to prove his point of worth.

After this has been portrayed, there is an expectation of a reward of love from his fellow man, an acceptance and respect for who he is through the image of his creation.

That is what mankind does. However, if you really look at it, there is an emptiness within the expectation of acceptance, which one calls love. For the folly of mankind is his need to seek the approval of others to reinforce his own value of self, so that self-love can be identified.

You speak of love as if you do not know it, and I believe you. I believe that you do not know it, or else you would not need to ask that question. You would know that, even if your relationships have not fulfilled your expectations that you have created, love was witnessed through the value of the sharing with another.

The only reason that you do not have love in your life, is because you do not as yet know what love is. Listen to this, you are magnetically drawing to you through the power that you are, the rejection process to enable you to identify that you do not have love for yourself.

If you do not love who you are, how can you understand love in the fullest sense through another.

You have asked me for an answer to your created problem, so that love can be visible to you. However, I can only offer to you my love, my complete love. If you can accept that, then you can accept the love of all who have come this day, those to whom you may never see or hear, but who have been drawn to you by the beauty of your light that you hide so well from the people of your Earth.

You say that you are not loved. Then I say unto you, let go of your fear of being loved.

Chapter 26

Q&A - Pain and Suffering

(Q: Could you give us a useful suggestion that can help us with the pain and suffering that we go through in our life?)

ELONIAS: You would like a way out of your tears and pain. Would you like the way or the hard way?

(A: Let's say the hard way then.)

ELONIAS: You would like the hard way! That could be arranged, perhaps we could add another twenty or thirty years to your life.

(A: Yes, that was my idea, yes.)

ELONIAS: That was not my intention though. You are speaking on behalf of each one here within this room, is that correct?

(A: Yes.)

ELONIAS: And each one here would like to know the answer, is that right?

(A: If it's beneficial.)

ELONIAS: Oh, it will be beneficial, believe me! But you may not like it. There is no easy or hard way. You just do or you do not. It is that simple. You hold onto your pain and suffering because you call it pain and suffering. Please follow me very carefully.

Within your life are many issues, each one of you, that will come to face you time and time again. As you face each issue, you will feel sad and lonely at times, because you believe you are alone with your pain. There are times that you are so unsure as to what to do with your life, and that is because you do not believe in your "knowing" enough. You are only working within half of your energy potential when you call it "pain and suffering."

Pain and suffering does not exist. Let us get that straight. That is what the self calls it, because it does not like it. When you see pain and suffering, call it "the greatest opportunity for growth".

Take away pain and suffering from your vocabulary. It does not exist, Only opportunities do, and when you look at your pain and suffering as being opportunities, then you are joyous. As you cry and kick and scream, you are joyous because you know it is leading you out into another acknowledgement that you no longer need to be within the fear of the denial of your light, and every opportunity takes you closer to "home". Home to that "what" you are.

Is it simple for you? If you cry, you cry with joy, If you scream, you scream with joy. If you curse, you curse with joy, because you know that there is a movement.

There is a movement away from the complacency of life into another avenue, and another doorway opens to you. Surely, that is a gracious thing that your illusionary pain and suffering can bring to you. Pain and suffering are the inventions of the self. Opportunities is what the higher part of you, the "what" calls it.

So, to you young man, that just spoke to me. Do not cry with pain and suffering, but cry with joy at the opportunity to recognise something. Whatever you create will be beautiful, even if your self does not like it. It has created it, so it can be recognised, whether it is needed or not.

After a while, you will work through that because you will not give to it the energy of denial, you will love it. All of your creation, you will love. There is no such thing as fear. There is only the joy of uncovering the remembering.

Please remember something. If you cannot see us, know that we are here with you this evening. We never leave you, it is only you that leaves us when you create your illusionary pain and suffering.

Within the joy of remembering, you will see us and hear us. We have never left you because we love you.

Chapter 27

Q&A - Fear of Dying

(Q: I have a question about dying. I have a terminal disease, and the Doctors say that I only have a few more months left to live. At first, I felt very angry and cheated that my life was so short, but now I guess I have to admit that I have fear of dying. Could you help me please?)

ELONIAS: There is much confusion within about the joy of "dying". Your anger stems from your confusion and your need to belong to another, whether it be a husband, child, or whoever.

When one views life, one has to view death. That is a fact. For within life, is death. All is a cycle of experience, and through that experience, the great awakening occurs of the power of light and love that you really are.

Whilst you occupy a physical body, you cannot see the beauty of death. For death to you, and to so many, is the enemy of life, that is ready to take all that you love away from you. Is that not right?

(A: Yes, I would agree with that.)

You are in agreeance with me because you want to believe me when I say that "death" is the birth into another awareness of life. You wish to hold onto the hope of a better place, a place where you will be greeted by those to whom you loved so long ago, Correct?

(A: Yes.)

To all who are listening to me, I wish to say, "The power of love that ties you to temporary things is not the reality of love."

By that, I mean, your fear of dying is highlighted by your fear of letting go of the love that you have for others. The unsureness of how they will cope in their lives when you are no longer with them. All seek to belong to others, within their hopes, ambitions and dreams, so as to incorporate a security of love. A love that will allow you to feel fulfilled within your life, That is a basic requirement for each and everyone upon your Planet.

However, when one is born into the world of matter, they adopt the acceptance of a "temporary stay" within a physical expression, that will allow them to relate and communicate through their requirement of love.

My dear lady, do not have fear. Do not have anger. Do not create an unsureness of what is the most natural experience within your life. For surely death to you is the entrance to a greater awareness of that "what" you are.

As you listen to my words, do not just accept what I am saying without acknowledging within your "knowing" that I am right. Not through your expectation of what you think will happen to you after the death of the physical body, but within the power of your "knowing".

Allow me to be the catalyst to your remembering. Allow the energy within my words to help you remember that you do not belong to this Planet Earth, but you belong to a greater example of light, that you really are. Where love awaits you in the fullest sense of the word.

Through one's conditioning process, great fear is issued when one speaks of death and dying. For mankind has been encased with his imagery of life, and through his imagery of life, he will never understand the true process and motion of death. Death to many, issues forth a precedence of anxiety and unsureness as to the "reckoning" of ones life.

Your various religions speak of the power and wrath of God descending upon each one when death comes, I speak of the freedom of awakening up unto the light that you are. With no image of love, but for the reality of uncovering that what it is within the higher reaches of remembering.

When your physical body can hold you no more, my dear lady, there will be many who will be waiting to greet you, to show you the way to that what you have created upon this Planet.

You have been given the greatest gift, the gift of returning home. One speaks of the gift of life, I speak to the gift of death. That is the difference.

Chapter 28

Q&A - Too Old to Change

(Q: I understand that change has to happen, but when you are getting on in years, like myself, you become set in your ways. How I see it, is that change will gradually filter down to our children. Perhaps they could be different than their parents. They may be able to make change.)

ELONIAS: You indoctrinate your children with your belief systems through traditions, culture and religion.

That is why black man and white man do not get along, red man and white man, Catholic and Jew, Buddhist and Moslem they all have division within their belief structure.

Your Planet has to change, for enough is enough! That is why we have come. Change is imminent. You need to step out of all your belief structures that create so much division.

You have not got much time. You only have a short period of time. And when you have your children as being little "duplicates" of yourselves within your beliefs and your pain and your misery, then all you are seeing is a duplicate of your power.

All is one light, but because you all see life so differently through your division of thought, there is a division of light. You say that you are too old to change your thinking, I would reply that you are very young in your understanding.

Chapter 29

Q&A - Mediumship

(Q: What is Mediumship, and what type of Mediumship is preferable to another?)

ELONIAS: When one looks at Mediumship, they are looking at what each one has inherited as their right. Your question infers that Mediumship is something that belongs to a select few, and that is not correct.

So let us look at the first part of your question. What is Mediumship? The value of Mediumship is simply the re-connection back to that "what" you are, through the image of the Great Beings that you believe connect to you.

I wish to speak of Mediumship without using the word as such. I wish to speak of it as being re-connected through love. Through being able to understand that you are not a physical body but you are light, and within light is the Absolute that you are.

Upon your Earth you register a need to connect to Great Beings that will deliver you out of your problems. Is that not correct?

(A: Yes, it is.)

ELONIAS: And in doing so, you do not do one ounce of work in investigating the power that you are. Within the reality that you are, lies the essence, and yet one does not see it, when they are trying to re-connect to an image of light. The Great Ones that I speak of do not come under the imagery that so many people give to them. If I was to say unto you, "Who are these Great Beings that you are all so keen to contact, to deliver you from your problems and your fear?" Why should they contact you? What have you done to earn the right?

And you would surely say unto me, "But Elonias, you have just said it is my right to re-connect back to "what" I am." That is true. However, you will never do it through trying to find someone or something else to bring to you the wisdom that you seek, so that your brain can become comfortable with more knowledge. So that you can feel important with the imagery of your light. That is not Mediumship, that is the image that many give to it.

We hear so many who speak of "Divine Beings" giving to them the answers of creation. There are no answers as such that the brain would be convinced as being factual. Many are caught up with the illusion that their brain gives to them of the importance of having the knowledge factor, which one calls wisdom, to come into their life. So I wish to turn the question around and ask, "Why do you wish to communicate with us? Why is it that you need us to speak unto you?" What would be your answer?

(A: My answer would be that I need it because I feel that your wisdom would enhance my understanding, and I acknowledge that I do not have that within my Being.)

ELONIAS: And why should you believe me? Why should you believe me? You cannot see me. You hear the words through this one (Diane). How do you know me? Perhaps that is the real question. For many are caught up with illusionary images that their creative mind has given to them. Do you understand what I am saying?

(A: Yes, I do.)

ELONIAS: And so they have a need to re-connect to their loved ones for example, in order that they know that they continue on. Some people are successful, and others are only successful in contacting a thought form that they have created.

That is very sad, because so many have created thought forms of their loved ones that are not real. For your Planet offers up illusion. Illusion in the sense that thought is very powerful indeed. So when one sits to contact Great Beings or loved ones, then we ask, "What is the intent?" That is the important factor.

For within your Being, each one, is the power of light that you are. It is magnetic. This magnetic power operates upon thought. Not thought through illusion, but the thought within your light, which is the "original thought".

I hope that I am not being confusing, however, I wish to stipulate to each one here - You wish to be a Medium, then I ask you "What is your intention to do with it?" You wish to speak to your loved ones.

You wish to communicate with thought forms perhaps, or do you wish to connect to the reality? I wonder which one it is, And when you contact whatever, to what end will it take you?

I have to tell you something that is important. Your Planet is operating within thought and memory. If you have within you the need to communicate through your memory, to allow you to contact loved ones within the Spirit World of your Planet, then so be it. You may be successful, you may not.

But my message is simply this. When you contact these Beings, that you call your loved ones, what then? The power of your light can extend much further than the Spirit World, and if you wish to contact Beings of Light, the magnetic law within you, which is within your light, will only allow you to draw to you equal to the magnetic frequency of your light.

For example, if you only have fear, anger, hostility and greed, then the magnetic law will only draw from the lower reaches of your Spirit World, In order that you can look at what you are manifesting through your connection. If you wish to go beyond your Planet and you wish to contact Beings of Light to give to you "wisdom" so that you can speak to others of the greatness of "life", then ask yourselves, "Is it for profit or gain? Or is it that your ego can feel inflated, with superior understanding."

Or are you doing it in humility, because the light that you are needs to connect back to the greatness of all. If that is your motive, then I am now speaking to you only. To the people upon the Planet Earth who's magnetic light is able to attract the Greater Ones, because of your need to bring that light upon this Planet with nothing for yourself.

Within the greatest humility, the power that you are knows that this Planet can be a wondrous place, and that many upon your Planet need to be awoken to the light that they are.

The energy of your magnetic connection that you bring to this Planet, will allow many, for the first time, to remember. To remember the power of light that they are, and that love is the greatest tool that one can have. Not the image of it, but the reality of it, and that the light that you are within the Medium that you are resonates a beauty for all to see. That is the greatest Mediumship of all.

Unfortunately, too many go into Mediumship with great ideas to find the truth, without first realising they will never understand what truth is when they are encased within the illusion that they have created.

We need your minds to be open, to not be cluttered with what you expect to hear. If you are intellectual, then you will never make a good Medium, because we have to pass through all of your reasoning powers.

Your analytical mind and brain. We have to cut through that, in order that you are open to new information that you will never find within the books upon your Planet.

Your question says "What is Mediumship?" All are Mediums, for you are all not who you think you are, but in fact you are a greater light. We are ready when you are, but we cannot contact you when your mind and brain is full of expectations of what you expect us to give to you to solve your problems. That is not Mediumship. That is the greatest illusion that you can manifest.

So simply, Mediumship is remembering that "what" you are by re-connecting to those who know you best. By-passing the Spirit World, for that also is illusionary.

The other part of your question, I believe concerns different types of Mediumship, and if one was better than another. Was that correct?

(A: Yes it is.)

ELONIAS: I would have to answer that by saying, "Whatever is suitable for your awakening is no greater or lesser than another method." If your awakening comes from your creative mind, then so be it.

If your awakening comes because you can hear something or feel it, as long as the awakening comes, so that you remember that you are not just a physical being, but you are the light within the physical being, that is re connecting to the awareness factor. Then there is no better method.

The greatest Mediumship of all is to contact the Absolute love, and to be an example of it, to all upon this Planet. Then I would choose that one.

No words are spoken, no pictures are drawn, nothing is heard in the sounds of voices or thoughts but the power of love itself. This is the greatest gift you can give to this Planet. That is the ultimate Mediumship of all.

I hope I have answered your question.

(A: Yes you have. Thank you.)

Chapter 30

Q&A - Karma

(Q: Could you speak to us about Karma?)

ELONIAS: Through the need to return back to the light that you are, comes the law of cause and effect. You call this law "Karma".

There has been much discussion through your religions about the value of Karma, and I would like to dispel some of the misunderstood versions of Karma.

Through the polarity cycle of negative and positive, Karma was born. The terminology has invented a reference to abide by for those who are struggling with the circumstances of life.

The Universal laws incorporate the necessary requirement of light to be instilled within each and every life form upon each and every dimension of existence. Thus allowing for the "retraction process" to occur, in order to bring all back to the Fathers House, from the illusionary journey of separation.

Whilst occupying your current space and time, you are undergoing an uncovering process of that what you are not, so as to be aware of that what you are. I hope that you understand what I am saying.

Rather than looking at "Karma" as being the adjudicator of your life, you should look at it as being the necessary component to issue forth circumstances so that you may uncover the illusion that you have created.

The reality of Karma allows the magnetic light pattern to maintain a cyclic reference to what is needed to be encountered. The law of attraction works within the current ratio of your lives upon this Planet.

Within your relationship to life comes a new sense of understanding when Karma bestows its presence within your life. Whatever you need to experience, through the magnetic frequency that you are operating through, will be drawn into your life so that you may uncover your reaction to what it has presented.

Many are adverse to the term Karma, and query the validity of what it holds. They try to steer away from the magnetic law of Karma by creating thoughts of "positive" thinking to offset any opportunities that Karma may present.

Through the power of thought many issue directives to enhance their lives, believing that they have overturned the power of Karma in their lives. However, it is not possible to bypass the power of Karma by applying superficial and temporary methods of creativity.

The personality, which is the self, does not understand the purpose of the Greater Plan, which is evolution. The reconnection process is completely overshadowed by the preconceived notion that the self has the power to over-ride the Universal law of cause and effect, which you call Karma.

When one creates an abstract view of life through the power of thought from the conscious mind, all that is created is more illusion. The self does not recognise that it has within it the power of light that needs to incorporate Karma into its recognition of its uncovering, through the lower frequency of matter.

(Q: Are you saying that we should not create anything with our thoughts? But surely we have the power to change our life here on Earth.)

ELONIAS: Where is your power? When you speak of power, I wonder what your reference to power is?

(A: All I meant was, that since thought is so powerful, surely we can make change in our life by using the power of our thoughts.)

ELONIAS: How little you know of the power of your light. You speak as if you know of power, but you do not. You are speaking about the illusionary power of thought. Thought relies upon memory, and memory only allows you to relate to what you believe you require in your life.

When we speak of memory and thought as being the power base in your life, you become very limited in the understanding of "what" you are.

When you allow the power to be within the self, you are only working with the limitation of what you want in your life instead of what you need in your life.

The self will never understand the fuller value of your evolutionary process, because it is connected only to the thought and memory cycle of the Earth. When the duality starts to operate, then you will recognise that the Karmic law is drawing to you, all that is necessary to be experienced whilst upon this Planet.

Chapter 31

Q&A - Responsibility

(Q: If we have no responsibility except to ourselves, and human nature responds because of culture to responsibility, what is the connection between unconditional love and responsibility?)

ELONIAS: We will have to break your question down, as there are many issues within the one question. "We have no responsibility except to ourselves." We will start with that.

What if I told you there is no such thing as responsibility. It is a self action that is confusing. What is responsibility, and what is self? I will put that to you and we will continue.

The next part of your question - "And human nature responds because of culture to responsibility." Is there not separation so far in the question? "Responsibility" is what one person calls it. Another calls it "no-responsibility".

When we look at culture, a set of rules are incorporated, that are man-made. So are we talking about man-made issues, or are we talking about evolvement of spiritual issues? Are we looking at the old method of understanding self with expectations, that are called "responsibilities"?

When you speak of culture, you are separating it still with responsibility. Responsibility is not an issue, and culture is not an issue unless one makes it so. Responsibility is a narrow thought that does not allow expansion of investigation.

Culture is also a narrowness of a social structure conducted through the ages past, by a hierarchy of people of that day, and tradition carries it through and you call is "culture".

Surely, it is a separation of beliefs and thoughts.

"What is the connection between unconditional love and responsibility?" Unconditional love "IS". It knows no barrier, it knows no boundary of thought and action. It knows no cultural difference, whether it be racial, economic. However, responsibility is a man-made desire, to stop one from investigating further. It is a self action of denial of the greatness of the all.

I would like to ask each one of you a question. What are you responsible for? Is it for yourself? Is it for another? Are you responsible to uphold your conditioning, your traditions, your religion, your beliefs. Do you feel responsible for your family and friends?

If you answer in the affirmative to these questions, then surely your life is totally caught up with the image of needing to be responsible for all that which seems important to you, to be upheld. All that you are being responsible for is the image of your illusion of being needed.

And one hides behind responsibility and thinks that they are doing well. It is a separation from the unconditional love, and therefore, when one is disassociated from that, one is encased within responsibility.

Chapter 32

Q&A - Obstacles in Your Life

(Q: Are there set and defined obstacles, and/or experiences that each of us must work through during our time on Earth, as opposed to our own personal needs and tasks?)

ELONIAS: What is an obstacle my friend? I shall start with that. Is it something that is opposing the relativity of going forward?

When one comes into a life, one has stretched in front of them issues that are there because of the thoughts in the past. If you see them as obstacles, then immediately there is fear. If one sees them as opportunities to be able to work through, then there is no-fear.

I wonder, my friend, if you think of life in terms of fear, or no-fear?

(A: Fear.)

ELONIAS: Then you have obstacles. Perhaps you could look at your obstacles as being friends. Yes or No?

(A: I try to.)

ELONIAS: You cannot try, you have to do it. Then we look at what fear is, The word "obstacle" gives to you a vision that something is in the way. Is this not correct? And when something is in the way, what do you do about it? Do you stop in front of it and examine it, or do you try to find a way around it?

(A: Try to find a way around it.)

ELONIAS: Does that solve anything? What about the next time that you came that way, perhaps it is a bigger obstacle.

Perhaps one needs to really look at it and admire it. Admire its beauty, and its design, because you created it, and it has to be beautiful, does it not? Of course. And because you have created it, and it is beautiful, you can stand for a while and admire it.

Then you look at it and say, "What joy I had in creating it, but what more joy I will have in being able to overcome it." So if we look at obstacles, I wonder if we are looking at fear.

And fears that you have are a creation of thought through time. You become aware that your fear has placed in front of you something to look at, and you call it an obstacle, but instead call it a friend. Then you can work with it and you will overcome it through complete acceptance with love.

You will find joy because you do not have to have fear any more. Fear is not a negative component in your life, unless you make it so, and you wonder why life is so hard.

Within your question you spoke of "personal needs and tasks". What are personal needs and tasks as opposed to thoughts and desires? It is one and the same, is it not?

A need, a desire, is a thought. Why does one have to have a need? That is the point in question. You can have several people here, and one has a need, but another says, "That is not my need." What is the separation value of need, and what is personal?

Personal is a separation of thought, through a desire of a singular nature. It is an expectation of desire, and it is a need, and one qualifies desire through a personality concept of expectation, in accordance to the rules of the day. I hope you are following me.

The cycle that you are on, is in accordance to a thought value of the past. You recreate your life through the value of the thought. As each thought is expressed, the delivery of action is immediate. You cannot deny that. So you are upon this Earth, on the "wheel of life", recreating that which you expect to go through.

You have with you the memory of fear. You are singular through your personality, your fear. However, fear is fear, and you have to understand what energy you give fear, through your own personal thought. And as you extend it through your actions and reactions, you allow your life to frequent that thought many times over. How many times do you need to work with the same fear?

The greatest fear that mankind has, is his lack of acceptance through another's eyes. Which equals no-love and fear. Why does it matter if you are denied, ridiculed and despised, when you are aware that the Absolute is the reality, and that your outer is responding to the frequency of love.

If you accept another's denial of your love, then you are equalling the thought to another thought of your own. Magnifying the original thought from no-love.

Many hide within religion to escape with their fear, so that they can find an outer representation through what they call "their God", to love them. They say "If my brothers and sisters of this world do not love me, then I shall hide away in my belief pattern that allows me to be accepted." Then they fight another who disagrees with their escapism of belief, and they call it religion, they call it culture, and they call it love.

Chapter 33

Q&A - What is Balance

(Q: Are we on the right track when we bring into balance what has been perceived the "spiritual way", with what we are now learning to work with, and that is our emotional and mental bodies? Are we being caught in another illusion, and how do we discern what is real and what isn't?)

ELONIAS: That is a very long question, with many questions contained within. Perhaps we will need to take it step by step.

Firstly, let us query "balance". What is balance? It is not one thing or another, for "balance" is neutral, and if you are neutral, are you spiritual? That is my question from yours. To be neutral and spiritual, is that on the track?

You speak of illusion. What is illusion and what is reality? I would like to ask you, "When you come within this room, and you sit to find balance on your spiritual path, what do you see?"

Do you see the illusion through the emotional responses, or through your emotional responses do you see reality? Let us look at emotional response in development of character, within development of intuitiveness, within development of whatever. Let us look at it.

What happens when the emotional part of oneself uses its influence upon your awareness of "who" you are? Does the emotional part of you create reality or illusion? I wonder if you know.

(A: I imagine illusion.)

ELONIAS: You cannot imagine. It is or it is not. What of the others here, What is your answer?

(A: Reality .. Illusion.)

ELONIAS: We have a few realities and a few illusions.

(A: I find it confusing.)

ELONIAS: You are unsure. Perhaps the point of reference is "what is the action?"

(A: Love.)

ELONIAS: Love does not have emotion. It is the expectation.

When you have emotion, do you realise that it is the barrier to one really looking totally at one thing. You are emotional because something comes to the surface that generates a reaction to the nervous system, that you call emotion.

My question is, "Is there balance within emotion, and is that your spirituality?" Is, in fact, spirituality illusion or reality? We could spend all night with these questions. I like that question because it takes us so many places.

So you have to, each one, investigate what is reality and what is illusion. If you allow the emotions to dictate to you, does it dictate reality, or does it dictate illusion? Does illusion mean for you something that is not understood, or is it something that is seen in a way that is not true? Or is it a part of both?

When people come together as you have, and you sit within a darkened room, or with your blinds pulled, whatever, and you still the mind, you create an illusion of peace. What you have really done is push down all your fears into the back-ground of the moment at hand. You call it a stilled and peaceful mind, ready to understand spirituality.

What is spirituality? That is my question. Is there balance within spirituality? Spirituality is a word that is too often used with an emptiness of meaning. Scrub it from your mind, and instead place within your mind an awareness of totality of oneness with all. It does not have form. It does not have a name. It just "IS".

It is what you cannot reach, yet you are working with the outer, and you are calling it the "Inner." You do not even start to understand that the "Inner" is the Absolute. It just "IS". There are no words or form that you can give it.

Spirituality is not a word that can be used. It is a definition of expectational behaviour. Do you agree with that or not? (Yes) It is a behavioural pattern that is deemed acceptable within a religious or social structure.

So if you are looking for balance within spirituality, good luck! I would look at it as a neutral aspect of it, because that is where it belongs. It is neutral.

So I have to place the question back to the young lady. Have a look at where your definition of spirituality is. What emotions that you have to contend with to find a light within the aspect of your Being, and what you regard as balance within love. Not the outer, but the Inner.

I now speak to you all within this room. The Absolute essence that just "IS" does not know balance, does not know harmony, does not know anything, because it just "IS". Balance means two opposing ends, does it not? One against the other.

When you have the Absolute, it does not have anything to oppose, because it just "IS". So you are really looking at balance within the outer aspect of your Being.

Do not confuse that with the Inner, or spirituality, which is a man-made word which goes with buildings that equals spirituality.

(Q: You speak of the Inner that just "IS", but what about our "outer?" If we don't bring a balance to the Inner, the two opposing forces, can we balance our Inner from the outer?)

ELONIAS: You have fallen into a very obvious trap. We have to look to what the Inner contains. Then we have to stop using words that have no meaning to them. The Inner "IS". That is the essence that you are. Is that understood?

(A: Yes.)

ELONIAS: But you are not aware of "what" you are whilst you are working through the vehicle that you are occupying on the frequency of the Earth, and the Earth is thought. All that you are on the outer is thought, that has been created through the ages past.

The Earth itself is a thought vehicle, and all that is within the Earth, and around the Earth, is vibrating at a similar frequency, in order that you can stay here.

The problem with mankind and his search for God, is his inability to understand that the Absolute does not need balance or form. It just "IS". You are not working with your Inner, because you would not have asked that question.

You are all within a body of physical matter because you are working through thought. This Earth vibrates to thought. That is constant and that is a fact, and whilst you are caught up in your creative mind, you are connected to the Planet of Illusion. Do you understand now?

Chapter 34

Q&A - Meditation

(Q: What is the value of meditation?)

ELONIAS: It depends as to whether it is a manufactured state of awareness or not. I was hoping that you would enquire more deeply into the area of meditation, rather than re-arrange the value of what it is to suit what your creative mind requires.

(Q: Perhaps I could change my question, and ask you to speak about meditation, and what you feel that we need to understand about it.)

ELONIAS: Are you ready to let go of what you think meditation is?

(A: I don't know.)

ELONIAS: Then there is no point in continuing, if you are not able to let go of your imprint of expectation of what meditation is.

(A: Yes, you are right. I have asked a question, and yet I am obviously closed to hearing anything new.)

ELONIAS: What do you want of me? You want me to speak of meditation, and yet you only require me to speak of it in a way that is comfortable to you.

(A: Yes, that is true. However, would you please continue. I am now saying that I am ready to listen.)

ELONIAS: Then I will continue. Meditation is allowing oneself to let go of one consciousness so that another can take its place. Would you agree with that?

(A: Yes, I would.)

ELONIAS: And so, by adopting a different consciousness, I wonder what your requirement will be of another level of consciousness. Perhaps we need to look at why you need to meditate in the first place. That is my question to you. For what purpose do you meditate?

(A: I am told that if I meditate regularly, I will be able to contact Spirit People and also my Higher Self.)

ELONIAS: Why do you need to contact "Spirit People?"

(A: So that I can hear and see them, so that they can help me in my life.)

ELONIAS: So your answer incorporates your desire to receive assistance in your life. That is your reason for meditation?

(A: Yes, that is so.)

ELONIAS: When you speak of the value of meditation, and the intent for meditation, I wonder if you can honestly examine the possibility that there is a more beneficial purpose for meditation.

When I say beneficial, I am speaking about the power of light that can be connected to, rather than receive instructions on how to better your life. However, for some who believe it is beneficial, it will be so, for there are many within your Spiritual realm who will assist with issues in your life. They, of course, cannot interfere with your free will, but through their encouragement and love, great gains can be forthcoming.

There is, however, another consideration for you to look at. The power of the creative mind can issue forth many thought forms that impersonate spiritual contact that you believe that you have connected to.

Many who are inexperienced in the understanding of meditation, go rashly into the creative thought form arena, and speak of great messages that are issued forth from a variety of "spirit contacts".

They are illusionary, because the person at hand is unable to change their rate of vibration sufficiently to instigate a connection to a higher realm of existence.

When you understand the true meaning of meditation, you will realise the power of the re-connection to those who are waiting to share with you the remembering of that what you are.

Many are caught up with the Spirit World that is connected to your Planet, and allow that to be the "ceiling" of their connection, However, I wish to say to you, that beyond your Planet lies a power of light that will instigate a "remembering" within you of the illusion of your life.

(Q: What do you mean when you say "the illusion" of my life?)

ELONIAS: Now we are getting to the "reality" of meditation in its truest sense. When I speak of the "illusion" of your life, I am speaking about the creation of your life by your thought. You use your thought process to establish an identity of who you are.

ELONIAS: So, through thought, you draw to you the environment that allows you to fulfil who you believe yourself to be. For example, your choice of partner, friends, work, where you live, and so on. Your thought is responsible for the well being of your physical body and also for your emotional well being. Your thought is a very powerful tool, that perhaps is not fully understood, but is definitely under-estimated by many.

(A: I see your point.)

ELONIAS: Your thought is also the "power-point" within meditation. Many use their brain and manufacture a peaceful environment so that their body may relax and they can allow themselves to feel very comfortable. Others battle with their thoughts of everyday life, and try to still their minds so as to create a vacuum effect, in order to be within a state of "nothingness". More fail in this regard than succeed. They become angry with their thoughts that seem to get in the way.

Through much frustration and various techniques, most eventually obtain a fairly satisfactory result. Some connect to the Spirit World, others to a creative garden or landscape, and others to the bliss of oblivion. They call this meditation. I call it a waste of time.

(Q: How can it be a waste of time, when you said earlier that it was good to contact our Spirit friends?)

ELONIAS: I have given to you the "small picture" that you can contact. This "small picture" will be quite satisfactory to many. However, I need also to bring to your attention the "big picture" that is available to be connected to.

When I speak of the "big picture" I am speaking of the greater power of light that can be connected to by the people upon the Planet Earth. So many live in the darkness of the illusion that the Earth is all that can be connected to, and that your Spirit World is the highest point of reference to be contacted.

I need to tell you this. The power within and around your Planet is very limited in comparison to the Universal power that is accessible.

Beyond your creative thought that binds you to your expectation of what is available, lies a greater energy that is waiting to be realised.

(Q: Could you tell me how I could connect to it?)

You need to be aware that you have within your Being a magnetic power point. This is the through the "note" that you are, and by that I am saying that all resonate to a sound, which we will call a "note". When that "note" is sent forth, it draws to it the power of the light that it is.

Within the circumference of your Planet Earth, is thought and memory. This energy of thought and memory, is the conductor of "thought forms" that so many are contacting.

However, beyond the Earth is the Universal note that you are able to connect to. By doing this, you will bring back a "remembering" that your stay upon the Earth is but temporary in the evolutionary cycle.

By re-connecting to the "big picture" of Universal energies, you are able to draw to you a greater part of "what" you are, and with it, the contact with the Higher Brothers of Light, who are awaiting to connect to all who are ready to let go of the limitedness of "who" they are.

I suggest that you do not allow the power of thought from your brain to do the work within meditation. But instead, as you relax your Being, centre your awareness on the fact that you are a Universal Being of Light, and not just an Earthly vehicle of existence.

By doing that, you are allowing your "note" to be accessible to a greater possibility of re-connection.

Meditation cannot be a structured and forced example of awareness, but it must be done with no desire or intent or expectation, but a "knowing" that you are more than you think you are.

The power of your note will then be sent forth and will allow you to register the Absolute Light from the highest possible example of "what" you are to be encountered.

This, then, is true meditation.

Chapter 35

Q&A - Symbology

(Q: People use symbology to explain their understanding of life. Do you agree with this?)

ELONIAS: You ask of symbology, and you ask in reference to factual appraisal. Let us look at symbology. What is symbology? Is it reality or illusion? And from whence does it come?

(A: Perhaps it could be the illusion of reality through our creative thoughts.)

ELONIAS: You speak of your Journey through recognising the symbolism and the affects of symbolism, and you try to put an intellectual response to it.

How can human beings who use their brain to analyse information, comprehend the greatness and the factual evidence of evolution? One thinks that they are of superior intellect when one can incorporate another's ideas.

At the other end of the scale, is the fallacy of disbelievers who do not allow their intellect to incorporate anything beyond what they feel is responsible and what they feel is factual according to their conditioning.

However, as we are trying to make ourselves more comprehensible to the human way of thinking, we are at odds with each one who is not able to comprehend that which is distasteful to their minds in accordance to their belief program.

Symbolism is a creative tale that enables one to move through a thought pattern of relativity that encounters a point of reference in order for that thought to be identified, and through symbolic references, the brain identifies its requirement of understanding. Symbolism has been used through your ages past, so that scholars of life can identify a similar framework of recognition, in order that others can identify it through their own personal requirement.

Whether it is "reality" or "illusion" is of no consequence to many.

Chapter 36

Q&A - Consciousness

(Q: With our consciousness, if we are drawing on memory from the past, is there a point where you can stop drawing on your Earthly consciousness, and start drawing on a greater part of "what" you are, and therefore stopping the need to draw on memory?)

ELONIAS: Let us look at the ownership of consciousness. If you look at personal consciousness, then you look at personal memory. What if I told you that you can adopt consciousness without owning it. What is the difference between creative consciousness, and adoption of consciousness from another aspect of your Being, in order to appropriate a new Program through a new realisation?

At any one time you can adopt another's consciousness, and you do it regularly. You hear great words of "wisdom" and you adopt these words as your own. You are regulating your consciousness in accordance to another's.

You draw from the memory of the Planet and draw from the consciousness to re-enact the power within your own. Consciousness is never stable, it is forever reacting and forever changing and re-connecting to another's consciousness.

To find the entry or exit through consciousness is what you are looking for, and where will you find it? Through your old consciousness of analysis and examination, as to where it may be, or through the consciousness of the Planet, without personal experience, of which you are not sure of anyway?

You want to go beyond memory, you want to go beyond consciousness. That is possible, but not through the interpretation of your present consciousness that you have.

So you have to detach from present consciousness in order to find the fullness of the remembering of what is beyond consciousness. You are really there anyway.

It is only the presentation of memory that assists you in being upon the Planet of your illusion, of your time illusion, of your space illusion, and through that illusion, reality is recognised. One has to first face the mirror of one's intending image to recognise the effects of illusion.

How often do you need the mirror to show yourselves the imagery? Is not the mirror the image of memory? That does not answer your question, but allows you to understand mine. My question is simple. "Why do you ask the question regarding consciousness when you do not understand beyond consciousness through the old consciousness that you are looking through?"

It is the old image that you see. The image that you see within the mirror is not the same image that I see. What creates the difference? Are you seeing the new reality, which is really the remembrance image?

This will lead you to more questions. Are you not aware that the image of your mirror should be shattered because that is not "what" you are. When you preen yourselves within your morning or evening duties, and you gaze at what the mirror sends back to your brain, what do you see? You see a physical reflection. You then use the memory of your physical reflection and you ask yourselves, "What is beyond consciousness?" Strange I when you have memory of the physical image.

When next you preen and primp yourselves, and you look within the mirror, try not to see the memory of your physical image, but rather look for the inner of your greater awareness, which is the light that you are. Understood?

So, you ask "What is beyond consciousness?" Are you not already there, and yet communicating through consciousness? If you communicate through no image, then consciousness is a by-product totally that is needed for the existence of matter, but holds you to nothing.

It is a useful tool, but that is all. You can slip in and out of it, whenever you wish. But you are not connected to it, it is just there to allow the body of matter to fulfil whatever it has to do. You are then mindful of being beyond the connection and attachment to matter and consciousness. It is the duality of frequency of awareness. Your vision will then be understood to encounter anything.

The vision of the "Plan" is where all is operational through the Greater Mind and "greater power", and consciousness is just a reminder of the attachment of the need of belonging to separateness and the power. What you are asking, is what you are already doing. It is only your image that is stopping you. The reflection you think you are.

The only reason that you are existing within consciousness, is because your brain expects you to do so. I will let you into a secret. As you know, your brain is needed for the functions of the physical body, it is the forerunner of knowledge and collects every scrap of information it can. It is like your "bower bird", constantly collecting, leaving no stone unturned. It allows the physical mind to create the necessary inference of expression.

My secret is this ... the brain is able to keep the physical body accessible for the illusion of consciousness. Listen to that. The illusion of consciousness. The secret is, that you do not have to be attached to it at all.

You accept that the brain needs to have current information in order that the physical well-being is able to connect to what it has to do, but you do not have to be a part of that, and isn't that interesting?

You see yourselves as the brain and physical body, and adopt the consciousness of ever-changing values, and say, "I am stuck with it." The body is "stuck with it", but you are not. You are the observer of the function of the body. The caretaker that can connect and disconnect, whenever.

In your day-dreaming state, you call it consciousness. It is a detachment from the mainstream of the brain's function. Do you know what I mean?

You are not the physical body. You are not the brain. You are the accessory to it. You are a caretaker of it, but that is not "what" you are. When you remember that, memory within the brain has no controlling influence over "what" you are because no attachment has occurred.

While you are attached, then you are connected to the brain and memory, and all other levels that can also connect to the memory of the Planet. All bringing in various Time Frames of memory. However, because you are not a physical body, and you are not memory, you are light from another dimension of awakening, you can detach yourselves and observe. The observer, that is all you are.

Chapter 37

Q&A - Death and Consciousness

(Q: Is death a process of re-programming?)

ELONIAS: Before we go any further, I wonder what your understanding of consciousness is. Are you, in fact, discussing the inference of consciousness from one consciousness to another, and if so, do you understand what consciousness is?

(A: Consciousness is where your recognition is at that moment. It is the awareness.)

ELONIAS: Are you aware of your lifetime as being one consciousness, in one experience of a human body, or do you see that consciousness can be of varying levels within the same body? How do you see that? Is there more than one consciousness within the understanding of what consciousness is?

(A: Yes. There is more than one level because of other parts of our self working.)

ELONIAS: You are confused. You are not aware of what consciousness represents. You are idealistic with inference and with its relativity. You wish to speak about "death" and you qualify your opinions through the registering of changes of consciousness to indicate death has happened.

How can one look at "death" when one does not understand consciousness. They are one and the same, It is in human form that one has a denial of exchange within the levels of consciousness that exist.

The brain operates through the consciousness of programming. You Call it conditioning, and the five senses that are programmed within the physical functions, allow the connection to what is relative to that particular Program.

That is called the "Human Creative Program" through the consciousness and manifestation of the energy of matter. Do you follow that?

(A: Can you go over it one more time?)

ELONIAS: No. I will continue uncovering it. The reason is because you are listening to it from another consciousness. You are listening through the consciousness of the brain. You are trying to find an analogy to place what is being presented through the knowledge aspect of the consciousness.

It is well meaning, but not very clever. Clever in a sense that one wishes the brain to connect to what is being presented, and one calls themselves clever because one has an understanding upon the consciousness at that time. Please respond.

(A: Using the knowledge factor .. ?)

ELONIAS: That is the consciousness of the "Human Relativity Program", that is the consciousness that mankind uses to bring about an awareness through the conditioning factor.

That is one consciousness within one body of matter. However, that consciousness can fragment and bring about a more collective response from the memory cells. Do not encase the Program of consciousness of matter, but clarify a broader spectrum, so within the physical body a duality starts to exist. Do you follow that?

(A: Yes.)

ELONIAS: So, you have upon the Planet at this time, a duality operating. The Program of conditioning giving way to an undercurrent. An under- current of awareness, surfacing because of the changing value system within the frequency that is now starting to operate upon Earth. This brings a greater awareness of what mankind is all about.

Therefore, singular consciousness becomes duality. Mankind has confusion with conflict, and that is what you are viewing now, The ever-changing pattern of consciousness. So you cannot look at "death" until you look at consciousness, and the underlying aspect of consciousness is, quite simply, thought.

So, my answer to your question of "death" is perhaps not quite what you expected. Do you understand that we have to start at the beginning? You might ask yourselves, "The consciousness of the physical form, is that living or not?"

(A: When you say living, is that the day to day motion of life?)

ELONIAS: Take it whatever way you wish. This is your consciousness relating, not mine. Allow the words that I utter to find a place within your Being. Upon the consciousness that you are, do you call it living in the broad sense of the word, not in day to day existence, but as incomplete in all aspects?

I wish to ask you a question - "Do you consider, through your evaluation, that the people upon your Planet are living?" Yes or No?

(A: No. Not in the fullness of it because of the limited use of life.)

ELONIAS: If you see a reflection within the mirror, is it living or not?

(A: The reflection is of something living, but the reflection itself is not living.)

ELONIAS: And where is the "living?" Is it within the mirror, or is it somewhere else? What is "living?"

(A: I am not sure any more.)

ELONIAS: You wish to ask these simple questions. You wish to speak of death, and what mankind expects of death. Then we shall do it properly. So, am I making you look a little closer at the illusion of living or the illusion of death?

(A: I don't know which is what, or if either exists.)

ELONIAS: Maybe it does not exist, Maybe there is no such thing as death. What is death to mankind?

(A: I was thinking about it earlier today, about what happens when the physical body dies. The body is worn out, but the consciousness is still going.)

ELONIAS: Just a moment, I shall help you look. When you look at "death", are you looking at "death" of the reflection of the fragment of the whole? If you are looking at the death of the reflection, then it joins other reflections in its illusionary cycle of awareness.

However, to use the term "awakening", then death is a different proposition. So is living. When you look at the reflections of the fragmentation, the cycle is endless. The reflections are caught up in the illusion of other reflections within memory. Do you follow me so far?

(A: Yes, I'm trying to.)

ELONIAS: Try to follow me until we get to the point when trying is no good. For example - I have something to take your life away. I have a knife or some object to strike you down. The physical body of matter ceases to function. The consciousness that you are resides within the consciousness of the reflection that you think you are, within the Planetary Program at that point of the consciousness. Only the reflection resides there. It is only the mirror image that is being viewed.

(A: Yes, of the fragmentation.)

ELONIAS: Correct. How can the reflection suddenly change?

(A: It could not until it was transmuted.)

ELONIAS: Then why does one think that one gets so smart when one dies? It will only react to equal reflections of the same consciousness.

(A: You only get smart with transmutation taking place and the fragmentation coming together.)

ELONIAS: Yes, that is correct, so "death" is illusionary.

(Q: Is that the fear factor of so many, that through the death of the physical body you would lose the frequency of thought?)

ELONIAS: Many who are trying to transmute through the consciousness, which is the lowest end of the spectrum, that we have spoken about, are trying to understand what transmutation is. Their fear of "death" is the annihilation of the power w1thin their illusion.

You have to be aware that you are magnetic, and you draw to you all that which instigates the awareness of separation. The Earth's frequency allows the magnet to be lessened. That is why you have a variation of experiences and all sorts of examples of human behaviour.

(A: I'm sorry, you have just lost me. Are you saying, "The vibration of the Earth, using the magnet as an example, allows that illusion to be drawn to it to recognise the separation?")

ELONIAS: Correct.

(A: So that in recognising separation, you can become aware to transmute, and transmuting is not reacting or responding, just being aware ...)

ELONIAS: May I interrupt? You are caught up in your intellectual capacity. You are trying to find a reason for it. No reason. It just is. One draws upon the Planet Earth that to which it needs to experience.

Therefore, if you look at the simple analogy of magnetism, it is the note that is sounded out to attract that which you need to recognise. In order to evaluate the separation, so transmutation can take place.

The underlying core of your lives has a theme equal to that note and that Program that you are. However, when the physical body ceases to exist upon this plane of matter, the reflection that you are then becomes more magnetised within the frequency of the consciousness that it is. I hope that you are following me.

(A: Yes, but tell me, where is the reality?)

ELONIAS: What if I told you that it was not on this Planet.

(A: That would be most comfortable.)

ELONIAS: Then you can be comfortable. You are, if I can use your term of phrase, "dead" to the awareness of the consciousness of where you really are. So, what one calls "death" is really the transference of reflections from one cycle to another. When the consciousness is able to transmute all that it needs, the reflection no longer exists, and then you awaken to where you really are.

(Q: So we throw out the reflection to experience the Journey of Remembrance as such. Is that what happens?)

ELONIAS: That is so.

(Q: You once said, "That the image that you think you are is only the imitator of what is not there." So would you agree that illusion is reflective of what is not there?)

ELONIAS: Is it not all illusion? Even your thoughts. You may have a thought on this day, and one year hence, you look back and use your memory, and you will wonder if you ever uttered it.

For within this moment in time, your thought is real, However, within a different state of consciousness, one year hence, all has changed. It is amazing how one is able to see the reality in one moment of time and a moment later call it "illusion". Is not life illusion, as you see it? I call your life "death".

(Q: Does that mean in the sleep state that we would return to reality because we would not be in the consciousness of the Planet Earth then?)

ELONIAS: Why do you not ask me - "Does all return to their Planet?"

(Q: Do all return to their Planet in the sleep state?)

ELONIAS: No, because some are illusion, are they not? They do not have a Planet to go to. They are just Fragments of the Aspects.

(Q: Hang on, you are saying that some are Reflections of an Aspect and some are Fragments of the Aspect?)

ELONIAS: Yes, that is what I am saying. Perhaps I am illusion. However, I can assure you that I am not. For if I was illusion you could not hear me. That is the way to know what is illusion. You cannot register an awakening with illusion.

Listen to that. You cannot register an awakening with illusion! That is your ticket off this Planet. If something is illusion, it does not register an awakening. That is a fact. Listen to what I have just said, for it is very important. All that is "real" in the fullness of reality, registers an awakening. All illusion does not.

(Q: When you say illusion, are you speaking of the Fragments?)

ELONIAS: Yes, that is correct. The Fragments that will not continue on to other Planets are the absolute fragmentation, that have been put out to experience so much. They are the illusionary vibratory field within matter.

It is a fact that many reflections from other Planetary frequencies do not even need to be here upon Planet Earth, but have given their consciousness over to the Planet in order that the "shift" may be assisted to take place. However, it is time for them to wake up, Wake up to that "what" they really are.

We have come to be the threads to your consciousness. To wake you up, and remind you of your "reality". As the power of "what" you are starts to register within the consciousness of "who" you are, you will fully understand your purpose here on Planet Earth.

Chapter 38

Q&A - The Past

(Q: What is your interpretation of the "past"?)

ELONIAS: Within the past is the reflection of the future. When we speak of the future, we speak of the "knowing" that all is not within the frame of the "now".

The understanding that is so limited, is the conception that the past is memory. The past only exists within the re-connection to memory, but is not memory at all.

When you look at time, as your observation through the past, you look at the regulation of memory. The past offers up an array of images that do not in anyway reflect the reality of the past. For when memory becomes the past, the image of the past becomes the illusion through time. I hope you understand that.

However, your question was in reference to my interpretation of the past. When you asked that question, I wonder if you understood as to "where" I am looking from, so that the past can be seen?

I doubt that you did, or else you would not have expected an answer as such. I reside within the image of the future. And you might question, "What do you mean by the image?" My answer is simply this - Whilst you are experiencing a separation from the "Absolute" through your awareness upon the level and Time Frame that you occupy, you will never, I repeat never "know" that the past, present and future do not exist.

The past, from the observation point of my acknowledgement, is within a recognition that it is, in fact, a lower note of awareness of that "what" it is.

Time through the illusionary recognition of the people upon the Planet Earth, centres upon the "tomorrow" as being the instigator of being aware of the "spiritual aspect" of their Being. The "tomorrow", which is the future, will issue up a greater sense of love, of light and of a divine recognition of their inheritance.

That is how I see that the "future" is recognised by the people of your Planet. However, when the past, which is connected to memory, does not exist within your complete "knowing", the format of evolution changes.

All the past represents, is the uncovering of that what "is not", in order that what "is", can be revealed. Within the centre of the reality of all, is the uncovering of the relationship to that what "IS". It does not lie in the reality of the future, but instead is found within the illusion of the future.

Whilst you are conversant with the division of knowing and not-knowing, the past will also be acknowledged.

Chapter 39

Q&A - Ancient Civilisations

(Q: Many people are interested in Ancient Civilisations, and are incorporating the customs and traditions of these civilisations into their spiritual awakening. Could you speak to us about how these ancient customs and traditions enhance our spiritual understanding?)

ELONIAS: A most interesting question, that I will equal with a most interesting answer. You speak of Ancient Civilisations as being the instructor of spiritual awakening.

How limited is your sense of acceptability that this is the case. How limited is your understanding of the light that you are. How limited is the need to draw from the past what you have within the now.

We would like to offer to you an explanation as to why so many are caught up with the Ancient ways and customs of civilisations long gone. This is because of the magnetic law of attraction.

This law is operating to allow the by-products of these civilisations to offer up the energy of the past, so as to "clear" the way for transmutation to take place.

Many are involved with the "spiritual practices" of long ago, which they believe will give to them also the power of the awareness of their ancient ancestors. However, within their memory lies the imprint of probability that they, too, are connected to the past through past incarnations, and they therefore are using the residual memory to reinforce and validate the need to once again be amongst the memory of the past.

(Q: I am sorry, but I do not follow what you are saying. My thinking was that the traditions and customs, for example of the Red Indian, allowed each person to connect to their spiritual identity. Are you saying that is not correct?)

ELONIAS: When you look at the memory of your Planet Earth, it has within it pockets of light and pockets of darkness. When we speak of light, we speak of the awareness of what the "Father" is. In reference to the pockets of darkness, we are speaking about the need to validate what the Earth has to offer up, so that self can feel more powerful within the culture and traditions of that particular group of people.

When you look at the limited cycle of evolution through the Earth's experience, you are only looking at a very small part indeed of what you need to uncover. Whilst many are using the Ancient customs and traditions as their catalyst to seek salvation, peace, enlightenment, or whatever, they are fooling themselves. For within these Ancient customs and traditions lies an assortment of that which is not of light.

One takes their history books and looks for that which they feel will make them comfortable when adopting the consciousness and the role-playing of a civilisation long gone. So they dress up and play the role of the past, but they only draw upon the memory of that which they wish to inherit, and so many do this.

If you call that spiritual awakening, then I would ask you to look once again at the intent and method that you use to uncover the light that you are. How foolish one is when they draw from the memory of the past and re-create the past into the future whilst adopting the consciousness of illusion.

Why does one want to occupy the memory of the past, when the memory of that "what" you are is available.

Chapter 40

Q&A - Dimensional Energies

(Q: I am interested in energies within a Dimensional understanding. Could you speak about that please?)

ELONIAS: Beyond your collective response of third dimensional reality lies a hidden and yet meaningful dimension that is yet to be revealed. Let us not call it the fourth, fifth, or whatever. Let us call it a level of "Absolute".

Beyond your comprehension of your physical world, lies an intense relationship with the building blocks of creation. You could look at it as a genetic relay stream of light. Genetic in the fact that it contains all available data, and within all available date, lies the code for life.

Building blocks of light are actually an interchange of a frequency mass which is highlighted through a structure of formations likened to a Grid structure. The density of these structures and the composite value is defined by the relationship to the connecting apparatus of matter.

The building blocks of creation beyond your dimensional realisation, are incorporating and highlighting a factual connection to the "Absolute" frequency that is coming from beyond the dimensional awareness of the Universe.

Let us first look at your Universe in question. Your Universe is composed of a structure of energy that constantly interchanges on seven Light Patterns. Therefore, there are seven dimensional responses to the building blocks. The Universal structure of light is sectioned into seven Light Streams. These seven Light Streams are inter-changing with each other at all times.

They are variable in relationship to the coding that is contained within the building blocks of creation. Just as the genetic connection to your physical body resonates to what is placed within the coding as such.

When we speak of coding, we speak of a great number of variable patterns of light. Each one being responsible to the level of frequency that matter needs to be connected to.

Try to see through your third dimensional "reality", your Universe as being in seven layers, each one composing a connection to the main stream through a value of the coding that is contained within all life and all light within the Universe.

Each level is connected to the other. Every level is operating on different Time Frames. So you would have, quite simply, seven Universes within one.

(Q: Is it possible that we have other parts of ourselves operating on other Time Frames? Is this parallel Universes?)

ELONIAS: Correct. Parallel Universes within one Universe. If you investigate Parallel Universes within one Universe through third dimensional "reality", then we need to bring in fourth dimensional "reality", because that is, to your understanding, the connection to Time Frames.

It is when you occupy the seventh dimensional Light Bodies that one can transfer within each level simultaneously. On third dimensional "reality", you are locked within consciousness that is only able to locate one frequency on one level.

You need to understand that the fourth dimension, which is your relationship to time, can be a barrier, but it also can be a gateway.

A barrier to the conscious mind when the conscious third dimensional "reality" tries to understand it. However, a gateway when it can connect to the new Program.

Through this connection, you will be able to re- connect to the "Absolute" that you are, and by this I mean the highest "note" that you are, within your evolutionary journey. Through this connection, you are able to by-pass all levels of this Universe.

(Q: If those seven levels are Time Frames, then does time exist in each Frame as to what we are aware of here?)

ELONIAS: Time exists only in the consciousness, Within the other levels are the awareness. Through your relationship of your third dimensional understanding, you view time as a point of reference.

However, if you see the levels within the Universe itself all composed of a different, I repeat, different structure of coding, you are upon the densest level there is. The other levels have non-existent thought forms.

(Q: You speak of non-existent thought forms, How can thought forms be non-existent?)

ELONIAS: Is not your thought unreal? However, through your third dimensional conscious self, thought is, in fact, real. Through another level, it is not. It is a reflective inference of time, co-existing with "who" you think you are.

The Universe itself is a structure of thought from the main body of the genetic line that it is connected to. The Universe is a seven-fold dimensional field of awakening, with many planetary systems within it, not just a few that you see or are told of.

Some levels have hundreds of planets that are beyond your comprehension of time. Many of these are sending their people, being fifth dimensional awareness into the denseness of the third dimensional Reflections.

(Q: You are saying that we are third dimensional Reflections, but we have an awareness beyond the third dimension?)

Correct, I hope that I am putting it simply enough, For simple minds, a simple answer. I do not mean to be detrimental, it is a fact. You are listening through thought, that is my difficulty. I have to use thought to relate to you.

(Q: When we talk about the levels of our Being, in relation to what you have just said, are they on the other Time Frames of the seven frames?)

ELONIAS: The other levels of your Being are beyond the Time Frames of this Universe. Please listen to that. They are reflected into this Universe. Because it is a thought Universe, it therefore takes on form and inter-reacts with that particular level of awareness.

I will put it simply for you. It is like seven parts of yourself, each one understanding a little different than the other one. So you are operating on seven dimensions of your understanding. One level being aware totally I another not quite so, and so on. Until you get to the lower end of the scale to which I have spoken of before which is the consciousness. All other levels have been transmuted. All other levels are totally aware.

(Q: So then, is the Spirit World a level...)

ELONIAS: Of total illusion. I will give you an example. If you could stand on top of a mountain and have seven levels below. Perhaps you could have seven levels of, let us say "crystalline form", that you can see through.

You have in your hands a mirror, and you hold the mirror up to the light and reflect to the top level the fullness of the light. This then filters down into each other level. The light loses its power and intensity as it goes down through each level.

You are upon the lowest level. Each one draws in the imagery of light through the reflection that is being thrown down. Once thought is operational, then it uses that reflection for whatever it needs to do. I hope that you are following me.

(A: Yes.)

ELONIAS: Imagine a crystalline structure that has its own mind, and the mind can therefore create the imagery of the light to what it believes it to be. It uses the light to create form, each one receiving the light, but in different densities. Your Earth, within the third dimensional reality receives the least. Is that understood?

(Q: Does that mean then that if you had transmuted the other levels ... you were saying that we receive the image of the reflection of light, that if you had transmuted those other levels, then you would be able to have a stronger reflection?)

ELONIAS: Correct. Which is what you have. Therefore, you are drawing the fullness through all levels of your Being, rather than connecting to the imagery of other levels of "who" you are. It is a seven part person that you are. Once you bring all the pieces together, then the light comes through completely.

(Q: So you wouldn't need to be on the Planet?)

ELONIAS: Correct. So you are bringing the seven levels into one. Getting the full light from the Higher Being that you are, from beyond the planetary systems of this Universe.

As the Time/Space "shift" comes into being, it brings all seven levels together as one, That is the Time/Space "shift" that all talk about.

If you see seven stairs. Can you see that? Bring each stair above the other, like a ladder, it will now look like seven boxes.

When the "shift" occurs, the light will shine down from the top of the ladder and allow each division to be transmuted, so instead of a ladder, you have a tunnel of light. Is that understood?

(Q: What creates the environment for that to happen?)

ELONIAS: Absolute light that needs to re-create and re-connect with the building blocks of creation of life. It means that a coding is disposed of to allow another part of the coding to come into play. One is outdated. It is called "The Evolutionary Status of Creation". It is the movement of light. I believe you are a little confused.

(Q: I was just thinking then, that when that takes place, and that light will be shed through that tunnel, what effect would it have on those who are not able to move with the "shift"?)

ELONIAS: It means that all those that cannot connect totally with all levels of their Being will feel that the "shift" is not real. They are not in line with the higher part of their Being. Therefore, they shall stay within the relationship of the frequency of their creation.

Within the frequency of "Absolute" light, we ask you to understand that within the seven dimensions of relationship to what you have created within thought, to the "Absolute" that you are, lies a variable relationship of light. The seven dimensional frequencies of awakening has to incorporate a total connection to a new Program.

If it does not, then it has to relay back to the old Program, for the new Program is not upon the same wave note.

It is likened to your radio. Someone has changed the station, but if you are unaware that the station has been changed, and are waiting for the same Programs to be relayed, that is all you will hear.

For the illusion of thought allows you to still believe you are hearing the correct Program, and all is related to the old wave note, because nothing, absolutely nothing can ever be annihilated. All energy is "reality" until it is transmuted and it re-connects back into the energy that it is.

(Q: I was just thinking. When you talk about Time Frames, and if time in itself is an illusion through thought, the "shift" has already taken place, but hasn't come into the consciousness as yet. I am just trying to absorb this possibility.)

ELONIAS: We are looking at levels of awareness. That is all we are looking at. We are looking at levels of remembrance connecting back into one. Because you are upon third dimensional reality, and thought is real to you, you cannot comprehend beyond thought.

All has a beginning and end with thought. Light does not have a beginning and an end. It just "IS". Instead of seeing it as going from Point A to Point B, look at it as an inward reality of many varying levels.

It is like going within a mist. The mist never ends. As you go within the mist, you are within the light. The further you go within the light, the more awareness you have.

It is the depth rather than the length. All light is only recognised through the depth, but in totality, it just "IS".

However, through thought and through the recognition of it, it has to be identified, and therefore it is understood by awakening patterns, which are called "Light Patterns".

You have within you a "Light Pattern body" that incorporates at different times, different frequencies, different shafts of light pertaining to the energy of the awareness. And central points within the pattern of light that regulates, listen to that, regulates the amount of light that you can take in on the level that you are, so you do not "blow a circuit".

(Q: Recently, you spoke to me and told me that I had one Light Body now. Is that in relation to what you are saying?)

ELONIAS: Yes, that is right. One Light Body means that you do not have to go through seven levels of your Being. Each one has re-connected back through the magnetic attraction into one, ready to receive the fullness of the note, which is the light frequency from whence you need to draw it from.

Upon your Earth at this time, many are re-regulating their Light Bodies to incorporate the dimensional reality that is to come. By dimensional reality, we mean that it will be known by the Inner Being what the major influence is.

If one has never connected to the Great Light through thought, then the bodies of light have to become transmitters and the receivers. The receivers of Light Patterns, which sends it then into the other bodies, and so an awakening within can occur. The conscious mind therefore starts to question its relationship to matter.

If it listened to people like yourselves, it would no doubt turn away, and dismiss what you have to say, for it is the brain through memory that is operating its awareness, but through the Light Bodies it incorporates a varying degree according to its needs. For each Light Body can only incorporate a regulated amount of light.

If you look at the outer bodies taking so much, then transferring it gradually to the inner ones, until finally the full effects within the physical body and within the higher subconscious mind into the conscious mind can be made apparent.

(Q: Can that happen when the Light Bodies come into one, or the fullness of light, can that only be drawn in when the "shift" takes place?)

ELONIAS: The tight Bodies have to come into one, or else the "shift" will not be recognised.

I have told you before that you are beyond the Program of this Planet. But you do not believe that, and that is why your conscious mind becomes confused and has to ask me questions.

If you really look at life, truly look at it for what it is, it is the greatest story ever created, and if someone wrote a story like that, no-one would believe it, would they?

How strange it is. I shall kill you because you do not love my God enough. I shall kill you because you want to keep your lands, and I need them too. A strange place to which you belong. There seems to be so many rules that become broken by those who make them up, and expect others to follow them, or else they will be killed.

(A: You can't win, can you?)

ELONIAS: Who is a winner, I wonder? Is it the rule breaker, or the one who invents the rules? I would prefer to break the rules than invent them, because the rules are only through the value of power, which everyone has, but has forgotten.

(Q: With our concept that we are working with in regards to the seven Time Frames, does that mean that we can't relate an awareness in those Time Frames to life times?)

ELONIAS: I wish that you would look at time a different way. If you look at time as an action within an environment, then you are looking at a modification of truth. You are looking at the illusion and not the reality of it.

Time Frames should be looked at as experiences of exposure of knowing, and not the action to experience the reaction.

(Q: Because all you remember is the reaction.)

ELONIAS: Yes, that is correct. If you connect to the Time Frames in its fullness of three dimensional "reality", you connect to the memory, do you not?

(A: Yes.)

ELONIAS: When you connect to the memory, you connect to the selectiveness of the memory, and not the "reality" of it. Each Time Frame is responsible for the awareness of the reflection of the light. That is all.

Everyone wants to know of past lifetimes. "Who" they were and not "what" they were. Why is that?

(A: Personal identification to power.)

ELONIAS: Yes, that is so. Why do they not want to connect to the energy of the experience of the "knowing", rather than the imagery of what they believe themselves to be? If you ask someone to look back into another Time Frame, they would speak of power or sorrow, and a number of issues they consider possibly negative or positive within their relationship to their greatness or their victim syndrome. Yes?

(A: Yes.)

ELONIAS: They never have a lifetime that they are not either a "victim" or a "Great Being".

(A: That's true, selective memory again.)

ELONIAS: It means that they need to identify with their greatness of their sorrow, but not their awakening.

(Q: You often use the term "Journey of Remembrance", is that the Journey of transmutation into the one of the seven levels?)

ELONIAS: It goes beyond that. It is the Journey of Remembrance of Light. "Absolute" Light. Beyond the Program that you are currently operational upon. It is the Journey back into the "Absolute" knowing through varying Programs of planetary frequency "shifts".

(Q: I have just one more question Elonias. In the "shift", when we draw in the mainstream of light and connect, then why would one have to continue here?)

ELONIAS: To fulfil ones obligations. The remembrance shall be shifted from the Light Body into the mainstream of your memory within your cell modulars.

Thank you for your questions.

Chapter 41

Q&A - Aspects & Fragments

(Q: Do all Aspects have to reach the seventh awareness frame, the seventh Time Frame, before they are actually aware of residue that they have left in other parts of the Universe?)

ELONIAS: Negative

(Q: Then are they aware of residue energy at any stage, at the completion of any note?)

ELONIAS: What is your comprehension of residue energy?

(A: That which hasn't been transmuted.)

ELONIAS: When you speak of transmutation, surely we must look at the Aspect and not the Fragment. Is it not the Aspect that is doing the work? Why are you concentrating on the Fragment?

(A: Because I felt that the Fragment was the representative of the Aspect.)

ELONIAS: The Fragment is only the by-product of the Aspect, needing still to examine the viability of a lower frequency. Perhaps the Aspect has left it there for a purpose. Had you not thought of that?

(Q: Can the Aspect then have representation on each note for a purpose?)

ELONIAS: Affirmative

(Q: Is that the pattern that it normally takes, that they have an imprint on each note?)

ELONIAS: Let us look at what an Aspect represents. An Aspect has a dual frequency pattern.

It is in touch with the furthest frequency of "what" it is, of where it resides. All the rest is a Reflection. Now let us look at Reflections and let us look at Fragmentation. There is no such thing as a reflection of a Fragment.

However, there is an energy insurgency component, and by that, we speak of the Reactor that is viable on the top note of where the Aspect resides.

This allows the Aspect to be in touch with the energy upon all notes that the residue operates upon and that is because the Aspect needs still to have a frequency upon the lower notes in order to sustain an example of understanding.

(A: Of course, because a Fragment is only one example of learning. So it has to have an example of learning on all notes for the full expression to be experienced.)

ELONIAS: That is why you will find Fragments on all notes of the Universe, so that all sounds can be recognised by the Aspect.

(A: It is also saying to me that the Aspect is in touch with its "what" the whole time, that allows that to be regulated.)

ELONIAS: Let us look at the "what" of an Aspect. Is it not the highest note of where the Aspect resides? Which is the top note, whether it be the 7th, 6th, 5th, 4th, or whatever.

(Q: Within one Universe?)

ELONIAS: Within one Universe. Or else you would be looking at a Reflection from an Aspect, which is different than a Fragment.

(Q: With the magnetic "shift", does that provide the opportunity for the Aspect then to dispose of all those Fragments, to eliminate them and the need for their experience?)

ELONIAS: Affirmative. Because of a new Light Pattern through that Universe which is viable. All levels of all notes, that is all that can ever be understood on that particular Program.

So therefore, it needs to collect back the Fragments unto itself because that Program has been completed.

It may wish however, to place them again upon the new Program because there was not a completion of the need for its experiences to be understood on all levels.

(Q: Is it possible then for an Aspect to move into the next Universe whilst still having Fragments in this Universe?)

ELONIAS: Negative.

(Q: So it has to have the complete experience within a Universe?)

ELONIAS: Correct.

(Q: Will the Earth always be the lowest note in this Universe?)

ELONIAS: Within this Universe there are many reflective energies called Planets. There is a cycle of Planets that are used for the notes to be operational. The Planet Earth is nearing the end of its cycle for the evaluation process to be operational upon. It has by-passed the existence process for its need to be able to be a component of energy of the lowest note.

It has no need to operate on the lower Program any longer, and therefore the Program of itself is obliterated. The component of energy of which it operates within will no longer be viable.

Chapter 42

Q&A - Fragments and Reflections

(Q: What is the difference between a "Fragment" and a "Reflection"?)

ELONIAS: Let us start at the beginning. Let us look at fragmentation. Fragmentation is the example of one aspect of knowing. An Aspect is an example in action of knowing.

A Reflection is a finer frequency that exists within a different realm of Being to that which it is.

To put it simply, one has to look at fragmentation as being "offshoots" of a realisation or uncovering of that to which it shall one day be.

Whilst a Reflection is adopting a lower consciousness in order to ascertain an influence on another level, thus the statement of a "mirror image", but not the true example of knowing.

Let us look at a reflection of a Fragment. How does one see that? In fact one does not. It simply does not exist. A Fragment only exists within the level of operation that is in touch with the frequency to which it operates within. It cannot adopt another frequency without the Aspect.

However, the Aspect, in fact, can send a Reflection of itself. You get in so much trouble understanding the difference between Aspects and Fragments. Let us look at the world of matter. The world of matter operates in dual frequencies.

(Q: What do you mean "dual frequencies?")

ELONIAS: Upon the level of consciousness lies the inert Program of relationship to what you would call the "Absolute".

The "Absolute" only exists within a finer margin of relationship upon the consciousness Program of the Planet Earth.

Earth is, in fact, as we have related to you previously, undergoing a "Shift" in its frequency, and thereby its Program is re-arranged to suit the new frequency of awareness.

Within the consciousness mode of the people upon the Earth, lies the unsureness of what their relationship is to the "Absolute". It, in fact, lies dormant within their current Program of understanding. Aspects upon the Earth are very few in number. However, there are so many Fragments that are creating the relationship difficulties of the ascertaining to what the Earth needs to progress to.

Within the consciousness Program of the Aspects, there is an awakening to a finer delivery of what needs to be understood. This is, in fact, being done from many levels.

Your problem seems to be that you are colliding with so many Fragments, are you not?

The world of illusion co-exists with differing frequencies known as "layered response". Let us look at layered response within the relationship of Aspects and Fragments. You are, in fact, within dual responsibility at this time. This is in accordance to the message of the Earth that dictates your responsibilities within your daily lives, and the response within the night time. Also within the day, when we are communicating with you, such as now.

You speak of the fragmentation of thought when you converse with the people upon the Earth. Fragmentation of thought only confuses the issue when one tries to find a way to become less fragmented. It is a cyclic issue, whereby many are trying to understand thought by creating more thought.

You come along and tell them not to think. They therefore think about that, and create more thought so that thought can be annihilated. I hope you are following me so far.

(A: Yes.)

ELONIAS: Back to the Reflections that you are. Listen to this carefully. You are forwarding a frequency of thought towards the Fragments of the Earth, hoping to create a by-product of understanding. You feel that this is difficult. And so it is. Now it is to change.

(Q: You say it will change. I wonder if you could tell us how this will be done. Also, you have just told us that many will never understand. Could you clarify these points?)

ELONIAS: The answer is simple. You will have to "re-connect" to the frequency of "what" you are, and not just the memory of what it could be, You will have to re-connect to the energy of where you are, and not to keep re-arranging thought to those who are so good at it also. There can never be a break-through when you are only speaking to those who will never understand.

Within the imagery of thought lies a diverse reaction to memory. You have witnessed that, and so along your pathway of illusion, you have endeavoured to assist others to look at illusion, However, illusion is all they are. They are not the Aspects. They are Fragments. They are here only for the Aspect.

I trust that I have given you more direction on Fragments and Reflections.

Chapter 43

Q&A - The Note and The Soul

(Q: What is a "note" and is it separate to our soul?)

ELONIAS: The soul is a fragmentation only of the Absolute, that is sent forth from the Absolute. Many notes are sent forth, and this Earth that you are living upon contains a fragment of that note. It is like a tune, many notes are played. The fragmentation is therefore responsible for the note that you understand.

Through the image of the past and the future and the now, you speak of a note as a complete item. I do not. I speak of a reflection of your note. When you can get back to the note of the soul, then you may leave the Planet.

To put it simply, the soul itself is one note. When you can resonate to the note of the soul, then you understand the completeness of what the Earth represents. You have to transmute your reflections into the fragmentation that you are.

One note sends out many fragments echoing through time itself, the illusion.

It is like hairs on a head. Each one composing a part of the whole. You are working with the responsive expectation of your note, which is not the reality that you are. It is the conditioning program of what you have ever been.

Listen to this, each one, You came within a body of a child that reflects the past through memory on another level. Therefore, the conditioning starts to deliver an understanding of its environment that it has drawn to it. Through its conditioning, it therefore responds through the memory that it is.

Through memory of past incarnations, it is used to fine clothes, good wine, or whatever, it would not be too happy to live within a dirt hut, would it? And what would happen? It would reject the conditioning through the descension, and therefore a behavioural pattern would emerge of rebelliousness.

It tries to ascertain the unfairness of life, because the memory is quite strong of responding to fine things. However, beyond the memory of previous incarnations that it has had, it responds to a greater note, and that is to transmute its need for wealth, power and great standing or whatever. That is why poverty was offered up unto it.

One can transmute all needs of material wealth when one can find harmony within no desire and no needs. So, therefore, you have two ends of the scale balancing, called transmutation. There is no response to having a great deal or not having, no reaction means transmutation. Are you following me?

(A: Yes, I am.)

ELONIAS: A little earlier, a young lady spoke of feeling "closed in" and not able to experience life in the way that she would like to. I would like to go back to that in reference to the "note" that you are.

Why do you react, young lady, to feeling closed in? Is it that you are used to a time where you could explore the 'frequency of life, and now you are feeling the responsibility a little hard for you to understand? Yes or No?

(A: Yes.)

ELONIAS: So you are divided with your frequency, one part of you wanting to ascertain an understanding, and the other part feeling it is not right to feel closed in.

You have on one side freedom, and on the other side the feeling of being closed in. You are two people are you not?

So for your answer. When you look at the note that you are, you look at all that you are. You do not look at the conditioning relationship of frequency. That is the imagery in operation.

Thought is allowing the conditioning aspect to find value in whatever form you wish to follow within a physical level of expression. You are within a body that is dross, you are within a body that is light. So your Light Body is the frequency of the note of the Planet. Listen to that.

Your Light Body is the frequency of the Planet, your physical body is the result of thought of all memory of all response and all understanding.

When you can relate back to the frequency of the Light Body, you therefore relate to the Program of the Planet, which is the transmutation of all thought.

To be aware of the inner light of the note of the complete soul, one would therefore recognise beyond the imagery of all people upon your Planet. You would understand completely the complexity of mankind's inheritance, of his fears of his no-love and you will have no reaction whatsoever, because you would allow it, because it is complete, and you are in total awareness of the note of the Planet.

Whilst you are working with the imagery of what you think you are, through the personality aspect that has fear, that has confusion and conflict, then you are reflecting a frequency to draw upon, that shall sharpen the image that you create.

It is like dressing up in new clothes and searching for a mirror to show oneself to. So you draw to you that to which you can see yourself within.

The law of attraction is perfect. Your imagery within the conscious mind would reject that. What you are running away from, you are really running towards.

(Q: If the law of attraction really works, if one is working with peace and giving out love, why does it seem that a lot of aggression is directed towards that particular person?)

ELONIAS: Whilst you have a reaction against aggression, injustice, unfairness, hostility, whatever, then the law of attraction is working nicely for you.

This is because you are still recognising the incompleteness in another. When you have no reaction, then you will have joy in all experiences.

You do not recognise aggression, it does not exist for you, You just have awareness that another is not of the same note, and the same understanding. It is when reaction ceases to take place, that the law of attraction can then find another mark.

Chapter 44

The Role of Elonias

(Q: What is your responsibility, or your job with the "Command?"

ELONIAS: You want to know the role that I have?

(A: Yes.)

ELONIAS: Within the environment that your Earth represents, you are well rehearsed with the clarity of thought and memory. We are responsible for assisting in the frequency of removal of "debris" from one's mind.

There is no separation except within the form that you give to me. I am within the energy of the Earth in order to establish a liaison with what you would regard the "lesser" and the "greater". The physical representation of Diane allows a reference point of human behaviour, to use the data of the Program of this Planet, within the consciousness. To therefore establish a connection into the upper reaches of the frequency of where I am.

Therefore, I exist on many levels. Operating upon your Earth through the physical vehicle of Diane, and also operating from where I am. It is like a "time tunnel", coming from the future into the past and back again. Except there is no separation except through the value system of where you believe I am.

I am here to assist with the Galactic Command Units. If you wish to enquire as to my importance or lack of, I have always said that I am a lowly representative of those who are far "greater" than I am.

I am part of a mission, which contains many varying frequencies from many Galaxies, from beyond your Universe. I am the connecting rod from what you call the "future", to what you call the "past".

I do not disconnect from the past to go into the future. Nor do I disconnect from the future to go into the past. For all is one.

It is likened to the analogy that I have given before. Imagine a corridor or hallway with 7 doors. You enter through the first door. You are within Room 1. You stay within this room until you believe that this room has given to you all that you require.

When you feel that you have gathered all that you need, you may go into the second room, but going through an interconnecting doorway into the second room from the first, if you follow me.

You then go into the second room. From the second room, you gain whatever you wish, as to how you view it. When you have completed what you have to do within Room 2, you go through the inter-connecting door into Room 3, and so on until you reach Room 7. These rooms represent seven levels of awareness.

When you reach Room 7, I would expect that you would leave Room 7 and enter back into the corridor. Is that what you would have done?

(A: Yes, that is right.)

ELONIAS: Wrong! You see, there is no beginning and no end. Room 1 is the same as Room 7. It is just that you expect it to be different. Room 1 is exactly the same as Room 2 and so on. It is through an awareness that it is so.

I am from your future. Perhaps you could call it Room 7. I am speaking through Diane, which we will call Room 1. But all is the same, is it not? Just the varying frequency of relationship.

Perhaps you think that I zoom through the skies upon some metallic type of ship, I would be exhausted going from one to another and back again. You meet with such regularity that maybe I would run out of fuel!

So where do I reside? I reside where you are. Within the frequency of awareness. Am I not you as you are me? But you have never really listened to what I say. The barrier of illusion is through the personality. I am a greater dimension of you.

I am in Room 7. I can never leave Room 7 because it is really Room 1. When I finish the mission within "this one" (Diane), then Room 7 will look completely different to me. For then I can complete another example of knowing.

When one learns, one really un-learns. Think about that one.

You are asking of me, what do I do? What is my role? My role is the deliverer of awareness, It is not to deliver awareness as such. But to deliver the frequency of awareness so that you can respond accordingly to that which you already know. I am here to wake you up, no more and no less. Then you can get on with your next stage of "knowing".

(Q: Do you have such a thing as spare time?)

ELONIAS: I do not have any, because time does not exist. I am or I am not. Whatever you wish me to be I am. Within the power that you are you will find me.

I am your strength. I am connected to your consciousness so that you can remember "what" you are.

If you choose to connect to that thread, then together we shall uncover the Journey at hand. If you do not wish to be a part of that thread, then so be it.

Enjoy your Journey, whatever you wish it to be, you have created it, so enjoy it. There is only one way back to "what you are", and that is to remember, to remember that "what" you are.

I am more than you realise. I am the power base to which you are connected to, and yet you draw away from me as if you do not know me, and you singularise your reaction to what you expect that I expect from you, each one. How wrong you are. I do not chastise you, I only love you, I just awaken the insecurity within you so that you can let it go.

How little you know of your own power, when you are so fearful of the attitudes of others. I care not for what others think of what I am, They will never know me, they will only know the image of what they have created, and that is not what I am, and so therefore I have no reaction to it because it is not a part of who I am.

That is how you need to live your life. Not through the image of others, or the image of what you believe you are, but "what" you are.

You do not even begin to realise. Your reactions, I hear you each one, and yet through your reactions I smile, for I know you are getting closer to me. Not through the fear of reaction, but by identifying the love that you know is there.

Do not be angry with thyself, do not be disappointed with thyself. Never stay in the wilderness for too long, for that is where the "Winter" is, and there is no growth in that.

A Dedication

Within this room we meet again those to whom we call in the night, those who hear the call of the Earth for help.

Within this room we hear your call, and we respond so that, as the joining takes place, the frequency of light is complete.

And as the brain ceases to question, we are engulfed with the knowing that all is well.

Within this room we wait no more, for we are together so that the Fathers Will is done, and the human will ceases to be in opposition.

We relinquish all fear. We relinquish all doubt. We relinquish all that which stops us from being totally aware that "all is one".

And as we now shift from the frequency of the Earth, to the frequency of the dimensional Inner, we travel as one through the knowing that what is to be revealed will finally be understood.

And so we release our bodies so that we can step within the energy that will allow us to experience the frequency that is operational, from another dimension, that we now take on as our own, and finally incorporating it into the physical body.

We dedicate "who" we are, back to the source of "what" we are.

Resources

Available Reading:

The Greatest Story Never Told
Amoen, Diane Swaffield

The Temple of Remembrance
Diane Swaffield

Upon the Sands of Time
Diane Swaffield

A Life Worth Living
Diane & Jason Swaffield

Available Viewing:

'The Illusion of Reality' Documentary
Written, produced & Narrated by Jason Swaffield

Online Resources:

eloniasfoundation.com
thetimecentre.com

Notes

196 ~ Notes

Notes ~ 197

Notes

www.ingramcontent.com/pod-product-compliance
Lightning Source LLC
Chambersburg PA
CBHW071430080526
44587CB00014B/1788